THE MIRACLES
OF GOLGOTHA

THE MIRACLES
OF GOLGOTHA

by
Homer H. Boese

BAKER BOOK HOUSE
Grand Rapids, Michigan
1963

PHOTOLITHOPRINTED BY CUSHING - MALLOY, INC.
ANN ARBOR, MICHIGAN, UNITED STATES OF AMERICA
1963

To my wife,
HELEN,
to whose love, prayers and encouragement
I owe so much.

Preface

The pages of this book are intended to set forth, in brevity, the miracles that occurred in connection with the death, burial and resurrection of Jesus Christ. Because very little has been written or assembled within the covers of one book regarding this subject, I have devoted a great deal of time to this series of studies which, I trust, will help us to appreciate the events that accompanied that great transaction which took place on Golgotha.

We find much written about the "seven words of Christ on the cross." But to my knowledge there is only one book available that deals with the miracles of Golgotha, "The Six Miracles of Calvary,"* by the late Bishop William R. Nicholson of England. That booklet is a compilation of six sermons which Bishop Nicholson had preached. Aside from that booklet, I have not been able to find anything printed in a volume devoted to that particular subject.

Because the Holy Spirit has seen fit to use the miracles, performed by our Lord during His earthly ministry, as parables to bring to us some wonderful and heart-searching spiritual lessons, I am convinced that the miracles which occurred in connection with His death, burial and resurrection should be equally instructive.

It will be noticed in the following chapters that I have listed seven miracles instead of the six which Bishop Nicholson discussed. He divided the miracle of the earthquake and its accompanying results into two chapters, whereas I felt that it should be dealt with as one miracle. Then I have also listed two miracles that he did not include as separate miracles in his messages. These two miracles are discussed in Chapters 4 and 5.

*Published by Moody Press, Chicago.

I cannot claim to have exhausted the subject by any means, as the research material at hand was limited. Instead of seeking to be entirely original, I have sought to give within the covers of a small book the general prevailing views on the various problems, as gathered from different authors, and then to offer my own conclusions. I am very conscious of the fact that there will be those who will differ with some of the conclusions offered. This should, however, not distress me, as I have presented my honest convictions as I understand the Word of God.

An attempt has been made to present this material in an understandable manner, with the average reader in mind. Though quite a few quotations are given from various authors, these quotations have been kept brief, except in just a few cases, where they are a little longer. In presenting the quotations, an honest effort has been put forth to present them accurately and with the real meaning which the original author sought to convey, and in no case has a quotation been taken out of its context *intentionally* in order to prove a point. If an erroneous view of any author has been presented, it has been unintentional.

My sincere desire and prayer is that these studies may be used to the glory of God by causing the reader to appreciate more fully the salvation which has been purchased for us by the Son of God at so great a price.

"Untold millions of men have died. Thousands have died the death of crucifixion, and tens of thousands of noble and God-like men have died as martyrs for the truth. But there is not a single death found in all history attended by such marvels as those connected with the death of Christ."*

Preacher's Homiletical Commentary on Matthew, page 638.

Contents

1. The Three Hours of Darkness

Darkness was the first in a series of miracles that occurred in connection with the crucifixion of Christ. Let us first look at the Biblical account.

"Now from the sixth hour there was darkness over all the land unto the ninth hour" (Matt. 27:45).

"And it was about the sixth hour, and there was a darkness over all the earth until the ninth hour. And the sun was darkened . . ." (Luke 23:44, 45a).

The events that led to the crucifixion were filled with drama and great perplexity on the part of the close followers of Jesus and of the Lord, Himself.

Following that agonizing night in the Garden of Gethsemane, He seemingly received an answer to His thrice-repeated prayer, in that, "there appeared an angel unto him from heaven, strengthening him" (Luke 22:43). This must have been a real source of encouragement to Him in the dreadful hours that followed. The mock trial before Caiaphas (the Jewish High Priest), Herod and Pilate did not by any means lessen the burden that was so heavy on the heart of this one who had done nothing worthy of death.

On the journey from Pilate's Hall to the brow of the hill, Golgotha, where, according to historical accounts, was the place of general execution, the lowly Nazarene stumbled under the heavy load of the cross. So emptied was He of His glory that He chose to feel the full load that had been placed upon Him. Under this load He broke down, and a certain man named Simon, a Cyrenian, was compelled to bear the cross for Him.

Very little is said concerning the actual crucifixion. Somehow it was so awful that the ones that have given us an account of it simply state the fact that "they crucified him" (Matt. 27:35; Mark 15:24; Luke 23:33; John 19:23).

This crucifixion took place at the third hour (9 a.m.). During the first three hours on the cross the Son of God prayed for His enemies, He committed the care of His mother to John, the beloved disciple, and gave the wonderful message of forgiveness to the penitent thief.

The *first miracle that occurred in connection with the crucifixion of Jesus* happened suddenly at the noon hour, when the sun was at its zenith. From the sixth hour (12 noon) until the ninth hour (3 p.m.), the Saviour suffered in silence and in the darkness of blackest midnight, in the night of God-forsakenness.

What was the cause of this darkness? How far-reaching was this darkness? What is it to teach us? These and many other questions arise in our minds.

THE NATURAL CAUSE OF THE DARKNESS AT GOLGOTHA

The natural cause of the darkness at the time of Christ's sufferings is not easily determined. In fact, it can only be explained by declaring it a *miracle*. When it is seen to be a miracle, the only answer for the darkness is that *God caused it.*

One of the extraordinary things about this occurrence of darkness is that it violated the laws of nature. "In the ordinary course of nature, darkness being the negation of light, it is light which is the antagonist of darkness, and which always banishes it. But the darkness of Calvary smothered the sun at noon! What an impressive thing."[1] In John 1:4, 5 we read concerning Christ, "In him was life; and the life was the light of men. And the light shineth in darkness; and the darkness comprehended [overcame] it not." But here at Golgotha, when the Son of God was crucified, God caused even the natural laws to be overcome in order to speak by way of three hours of darkness.

[1] William R. Nicholson, *The Six Miracles of Calvary,* page 20.

There have been attempts made to convince man that the darkness was caused by a natural eclipse of the sun, such as the earth experiences when the moon passes directly between the sun and the earth, and that the only miraculous element is found in the timing of the eclipse. They contend that it was a miracle that it happened precisely when Christ was crucified, but otherwise that it was caused by natural laws of nature.

Many scholars are agreed that this could not have been a natural eclipse. "Since it was the time of full moon . . . it seems only in accordance with the evangelist's narrative to regard the occurrence of the event as supernatural."[2] "The charge that it was a natural eclipse is put into the mouths of the Jews in the *Acts of Pilate,* contained in the pseudo gospel of Nicodemus."[3] Hastings also quotes G. T. Purves as saying, "There is no need to interpret Luke as an eclipse in an astronomical sense. It is simply a statement that the sun's light failed."[4]

Let me also quote Frederick W. Farrar. "It could have been no darkness of any natural eclipse, for the Paschal moon was at the full; but it was one of those 'signs from heaven' for which, during the ministry of Jesus, the Pharisees had so often clamored in vain."[5] Truly, this should have satisfied the antagonistic Pharisees, but still Christ said that the only true sign of His deity and authority would be the sign of Jonah (Matt. 12:38-40, cf. John 2:18, 19, 21), that is, His physical resurrection from the grave. What effect this darkness had upon these sign-seeking Pharisees, we do not know. But we do know that it caused some of the soldiers, one in particular, to declare, "Truly this was the Son of God" (Matt. 27:54).

Going back into earlier historical records, we find that "Julius Africann (A.D. 220) in his *Chronica* opposes the

[2] Alfred Edersheim, *The Life and Times of Jesus, the Messiah,* Vol. 2, page 604.
[3] James Hastings, *A Dictionary of the Bible,* Vol. 1, page 559.
[4] *Ibid.,* page 559.
[5] *The Life of Christ,* page 647.

heathen historian, Thallum, for explaining the darkness as
an eclipse, which at the Passover would be impossible."[6] If
it had been a natural eclipse, it would have only lasted a
few minutes, and would not have been sudden darkness as
this seemingly was.

THE EXTENT OF THE DARKNESS

It has been a point of controversy with many as to how
far-reaching the darkness was. Some feel that it was localized, that is, confined to the Palestinian or Judean area.
Others believe that there was darkness covering the half of
the globe on which the sun was at that time shining, thus
causing darkness over the whole earth.

There is some real question as to the authenticity of some
of the ancient records that are available concerning this
darkness. In some cases it seems as if they were written to discredit the accuracy of the Biblical account, or others stretch
things to give credence to the Gospel records. However, I do
want to point out a few of these non-Biblical accounts to
show that there are ancient records that do record what
could possibly be this darkness.

"The primitive fathers, as for instance Origen and Eusebius, were acquainted with heathen records, some of which
were from distant countries, such as that of Phlegon, a freed-
man of the Emperor Adrian, which mentions an eclipse of
the sun at the same time with the crucifixion of Christ, and
that one so entire, terrific and wonderful had never before
been seen in the world. The ancient tradition also states that
Diogenes witnessed, in Egypt, the solar darkness which preceded the death of Jesus, and exclaimed, 'Either the Deity
Himself suffers at this moment, or sympathizes with one
that does.' "[7]

"Origen (in *Con. Cels.* II. 33, 59; comp. 14) tells us that
Phlegon recorded an earthquake and the darkness in his

---

[6] Alfred Plummer, *The International Critical Commentary* on Luke,
page 536.
[7] F. W. Krummacher, *The Suffering Saviour*, page 379.

Chronicles. Eusebius in the Chronicles quotes the words of Phlegon, stating that in the 202nd Olympiad there was a very great eclipse; also that there was a great earthquake in Bithynia, which destroyed a great part of Nicea. It is impossible to determine whether the events recorded by Phlegon have any connection with the phenomena which accompanied the death of Christ."[8]

Let us also look at a quotation from Phlegon, who lived in the second century after Christ. His writings are questioned by some critics, but here again, I believe that there is possibly some added light given regarding the darkness that occurred at the crucifixion of Christ. "In the fourth year of the 202nd Olympiad, there was an extraordinary eclipse of the sun; at the sixth hour; the day was turned into dark night, so that the stars in heaven were seen: and there was an earthquake in *Bithynia,* which overthrew many houses in the city of Nice."[9] One difficulty we have with the above quotation is that some records differ in the exact wording of it. Nothing is said of Judea, nor the extent or duration of the darkness.

Thallus speaks of a "darkness over all the world, and an earthquake which threw down many houses in Judea and in other parts of the earth."[10] However, critics put little confidence in this statement.

Though the accuracy of these ancient records cannot be fully substantiated, they do throw added light on the fact that something extraordinary did happen, which possibly was the event that occurred at Christ's crucifixion and death. There is no reason to discredit historians for their records, for such an extraordinary event would get the attention of many notables. The only difficulty we have is that of checking the authenticity of these records.

This, however, still does not answer the question, "How far did this darkness reach?"

Let us turn again to the Biblical account. Matthew says

---

8 Plummer, *op. cit.,* page 536.
9 Quoted from *Clarke's Commentary,* Vol. 5, page 276.
10 *Ibid.,* quoted from page 276.

(27:45), "Now from the sixth hour there was darkness *over all the land* unto the ninth hour." Luke declares (23:44), "There was darkness *over all the earth* until the ninth hour." Again, Mark writes (15:33), "There was darkness *over the whole land.*"

Ferdinand Prat feels that by the fact that mention was made of the precise hour, the evangelists give us to understand that there is no question but that it was only a local phenomenon, because the hours around the world vary according to meridians. He further contends that the sign was of interest to Judea, where it could be understood, for it would have no significance to others.[11]

The reason given by Prat for why he feels that darkness was localized is the fact that the words "over all the land," "all the earth," and "over the whole land," would seemingly refer to the local area. Matthew, Mark or Luke are agreed in writing EPI PASAN (or HOLEN) TĒN GĒN. But GĒ does not necessarily mean the local area. In fact, Thayer says concerning the word, GĒ, that it "refers to a specific land only when it is plain from the context *what land is meant.*"[12]

This same word is used by Luke in Acts 1:8 where he quotes Christ as saying, ". . . and unto the *uttermost* parts of the *earth.*" Even to where the darkness had been, there the glory of the gospel must also shine forth.

Hebrews 11:13, speaking of the patriarchs, says, they "confessed that they were strangers and pilgrims on the *earth.*" Here again GĒ is employed.

To this agrees R. C. H. Lenski when he says, GĒ cannot here mean only 'land' or 'country.' . . . The fact that this darkness covered 'the whole earth' or 'all the earth' ought to be disputed no longer. When the light of the sun is shut off, the day-half of the globe is made dark."[13] Luke (23:45) states, "The sun was darkened," thus stating that the cause of this phenomenal darkness was *in the sun itself.* Samuel

---

[11] *Jesus and His Life, His Teaching and His Work,* Vol. 2, pages 396, 397.

[12] *Thayer's Greek-English Lexicon of the New Testament,* page 115.

[13] *The Interpretation of Saint Mark's Gospel,* page 713.

J. Andrews states that Alford was of the conviction that the darkness covered all the parts of the earth where the sun was then shining.[14] Also, historical records indicate that many of the Church Fathers spoke of the darkness as being universal. "Tertullian says that a notice of this darkness was to be found in the archives of Rome (*Apol.* XXI),"[15] but here again, we cannot trace with full certainty the accuracy of this record.

Farrar points out that the early Church Fathers appealed to pagan authorities (the historian Phalles, the chronicler Phlegon) regarding such darkness as mentioned in the Gospel account, "but we have no means of testing the accuracy of these references, and it is quite possible that the darkness was a local gloom, which hung densely over the guilty city and its immediate neighborhood. . . ."[16]

There is one more reason for the belief that this appalling darkness was not just localized, but was a universal darkness. Since the darkness was, to a great extent, symbolical of the spiritual darkness through which Christ went for the whole world (we shall speak more of this later), it follows that this darkness must have been universal. The day-half of the globe was shut up in darkness because the sun was darkened. But you might say, "How did it affect the other half of the globe?" It was already dark because it was night.

Let me refer you to two Old Testament prophecies, which probably have a yet future fulfilment when God will take vengeance on those who obey not His gospel. Yet, because the death of Christ was the judgment for the sins of the world, these same signs accompanied His death. We read in Isaiah 13:10, "For the stars of heaven and the constellations thereof shall not give their light: the sun shall be darkened in his going forth, and the moon shall not cause her light to shine." Also read Joel 3:15, "The sun and moon shall be darkened, and the stars shall withdraw their shining."

It being full moon on the day of the passover, the sun

---

[14] *The Life of Our Lord Upon The Earth,* p. 544, 545.
[15] *Pulpit Commentary on Matthew,* Vol. 2, page 592.
[16] Farrar, *op. cit.,* page 647.

and the moon were both shining but on the opposite half of the earth. There was no place where one of the two was not shining. When the sun was darkened, the sun failed to give forth its light, thus the moon, which is but a reflection of the sun, also became totally dark. The impact of this darkness was thus felt by the whole earth.

This darkness that accompanied the crucifixion of Jesus was a miracle. It was of divine origin. Because of the significance, one is almost compelled to conclude that the darkness extended over the entire earth.

OCCURRENCES OF DARKNESS IN THE SCRIPTURES

In order to get the proper understanding of the darkness which occurred the day our Saviour died, it would be helpful to consider other occasions where there was darkness upon the earth. An understanding of the meaning of a word in the Bible is frequently gained by going to the first place that word is used in the Bible, and finding its meaning and usage there. It often gives the key to the use of that word elsewhere.

We have two other occasions in the Bible where there was a special *darkness* upon the earth besides the one at Christ's crucifixion. When these three occasions are compared, it will be noticed that the basic cause of the darkness is similar.

The first occurrence of darkness is found in the very beginning of the Bible, in the Genesis (1:2) account of creation. "In the beginning God created the heaven and the earth. And the earth was without form, and void; and *darkness* was upon the face of the deep."

The second time our attention is called to an awful darkness is recorded in Exodus 10:21, 22, the occurrence of the ninth plague or judgment upon Egypt and upon Pharaoh because they would not let God's people, Israel, go free to worship the Lord God, the Eternal "I AM." "And the Lord said unto Moses, Stretch out thine hand toward heaven, that there may be *darkness* over the land of Egypt, even *darkness* which shall be felt. And Moses stretched forth his hand

toward heaven; and there was a *thick darkness* in the land
of Egypt three days."

In all three cases it seems that the darkness carries with
it the same significance — an expression of a Holy God
extremely displeased with sin. It will be observed that in all
three cases there was an appalling darkness which was followed by light of redemption.

It should be helpful to consider the first two occasions
of darkness, which I believe will throw light on the third
occasion.

It is quite commonly believed that the chaos and darkness
in the Genesis account of creation is not a part of God's
original creation — that is, that God did not create it in a
chaotic condition. But rather, the chaos and darkness are a
direct result of Divine judgment. It would appear that some
kind of catastrophe took place between verses one and two.
From various intimations in other places in the Old Testament, it is held by some Bible scholars that what happened
between verses one and two is what we find recorded in
Isaiah 14:9-14 and Ezekiel 28:12-15; that is, Lucifer, one of
the created cherubs of God, was cast out of the presence of
God, down to the earth. As he was cast down to the earth, the
earth became the subject of judgment, and possibly that is
what Isaiah had in mind when he wrote (Isa. 24:1), "Behold, the Lord maketh [not referring to original creation]
the earth empty, and maketh it waste and turneth it upside
down." It would appear that Isaiah was referring to a special
act of judgment by God. The Scofield reference Bible in
a footnote on Genesis 1:2 says that the earth bears evidence
that such a catastrophe took place at one time.

It would be of interest to note what Isaiah says (45:18)
concerning God's creation of the earth. "God himself that
formed the earth and made it; he hath established it, he created [original act] it not in vain [TOHUW — meaning void],
He formed it to be inhabited." In the phrase, "He created it
not in vain," the word vain (TOHUW) means the same as
the word void (BOHUW), meaning "to lie waste, a desola-

tion, empty, without form.[17] Thus, Isaiah 45:18 says that
"God himself . . . created it not void." Why then does Genesis
1:2 say, "And the earth was without form, and void; and
darkness was up the face of the deep"?

After God created the world, not empty and void, nor
covered with darkness, but rather perfect, as all that He has
ever done is perfect, Lucifer, the angel of light, rebelled
against God, and sought to elevate himself to be equal with
God. Because of this rebellion he was thrust from the presence of God, as we previously mentioned, and was cast to
the earth. Because he was cast to the earth, the earth became
a chaos and full of darkness as a Divine judgment against
the throne of the wicked one. That is when the earth became
empty and void, and thus the earth was turned upside down
(Isa. 24:1).

The rest of Genesis 1 speaks of God's recreative act.

It seems quite evident that the darkness in Genesis 1:2 was
caused by the origin of sin between verses 1 and 2. Thus the
darkness is a definite token of judgment.

In Exodus 10:21, 22, it is again â darkness of judgment.
The children of Israel, God's chosen people, were being held
in bondage in Egypt. God had raised up a leader by the
name of Moses whom He had preserved during the days that
all male children were being killed (Ex. 2). He had permitted him to be trained in the schools of Egypt. His final
schooling was in the school of the wilderness, where for
forty years he cared for his father-in-law's sheep. It was from
this lowly task that Moses was called of God to deliver the
children of Israel from the hands of their oppressors.

When Moses appeared before Pharaoh, the prince of
Egypt would not consent to let his subjects go. That was the
beginning of a series of judgments that came upon the land
of Egypt and Pharaoh. The judgments increased in intensity
until, in the ninth plague, God caused great darkness to
cover the land of Egypt for three days. This darkness was so

---

17 *Strong's Hebrew Lexicon.*

intense that it could be felt. It is interesting to note that this by no means softened the hard heart of wicked Pharaoh.

The above two instances are given to show that when darkness did occur, it was a measure of judgment sent from God. Thus the darkness at Golgotha, which apparently covered the whole world, declares to us that judgment was upon Jesus, which is in accord with the over-all teaching of the Scriptures concerning His death. Why was it upon Him, when He had no sin? He had no sin of His own, but He had our sins upon Him and He was bearing our judgment.

USE OF THE WORD *DARKNESS*

"In the Bible the main use of darkness is in contrast to light. Light is the symbol of God's purity, wisdom and glory. Darkness is the opposite."[18] There are a number of uses in the Bible for which the word "darkness" is employed. The following list of references is by no means exhaustive, but in each of these we can see, to some degree, its connection with the darkness that God sent during the crucifixion.

It is used as an expression of trouble and affliction. David, in the midst of his conflict with the Philistines, wrote in his song of deliverance (II Sam. 22:29), "For thou art my Lamp, O Lord, and the Lord will lighten my darkness [or affliction]." Eliphaz, in his discourse with Job, says that the froward "meet with darkness in the daytime, and grope in the noonday as in the night" (Job 5:14). Truly, the darkness that overcame Christ at Golgotha was a time of trouble and distress.

Darkness is used to express human ignorance. Job declares (19:8), "He hath fenced up my way that I cannot pass and he hath set darkness in my path." In I John 2:11 we read, "He that hateth his brother is in darkness, and walketh in darkness, and knoweth not whither he goeth, because the darkness hath blinded his eyes."

The word "darkness" is further employed to depict the moral depravity of man. Jesus said in John 3:19, "And this

---

[18] *International Standard Bible Encyclopedia,* Vol. 2, page 789.

is the condemnation, that light is come into the world, and men loved darkness rather than light because their deeds were evil." Or, as we read in Romans 13:12, "The night is far spent, the day is at hand: let us therefore put off the works of darkness, and let us put on the armour of light."

Then, as we study the Scriptures, we become mindful of the fact that darkness is used symbolically of punishment and judgment. The prophet Zephaniah, speaking about the wickedness of Judah, and of the judgment that was to come, says, (1:15) "That day is a day of wrath, a day of trouble and distress, a day of wasteness and desolation, a day of *darkness* and gloominess, a day of clouds and thick darkness." The prophet Ezekiel, in speaking out against the Pharaoh of Egypt in the days of the captivity of Judah in Babylon, sends forth his warning in the following words (32:7, 8), "And when I shall put thee out, I will cover the heaven, and make the stars thereof *dark;* I will cover the sun wth a cloud, and the moon shall not give her light. All the bright lights of heaven will I make dark over thee, and set *darkness* upon thy hand, saith the Lord God."

Judgment in the preceding verses is portrayed as darkness. That seems to be the basic meaning of the darkness at the time of the crucifixion, though it may have had other implications, as we shall see a little later.

The day when God judges sin is always a day of darkness. It was such for the world when Satan was cast out from the throne of God. It was thus for Israel and the heathen nations in the past. It was darkness for Christ when He died that awful death for us. It will be such for all who reject this Sufferer as their Saviour. Yea, the tragic thing is that even now all unbelievers are under the wrath (John 3:36), not because God wants them there, as He "is not willing that any should perish, but that all should come to repentance" (II Peter 3:9), but they are under the wrath because they refuse to come out from under that condemnation. Christ came "not to condemn the world, but that the world through him might be saved" (John 3:17).

We quoted Zephaniah 1:15, above, to show that all of

God's judgments are darkness. Joel, one of the earliest writing prophets, devoting most of his prophecies to judgment in the immediate future of his day and of the "end time" says (2:1, 2), "Blow ye the trumpet in Zion, and sound an alarm in my holy mountain; let all the inhabitants of the land tremble: for the day of the Lord cometh, for it is nigh at hand; a day of *darkness* and of gloominess, a day of clouds and of *thick darkness,* as the morning spread upon the mountains. . . ." Also verse 31, "The sun shall be turned into *darkness,* and the moon into blood, before the great and terrible day of the Lord come."

Amos, the prophet of the Northern Kingdom, declared the burden of Jehovah over the sin and light-heartedness of Israel in saying (5:18, 20), "Woe unto you that desire the day of the Lord! . . . the day of the Lord is *darkness,* and not light. . . . Shall not the day of the Lord be darkness, and not light? even very *dark,* and no brightness in it?"

In the book of the Revelation where we have a list of the awful judgments that are to come upon the earth before Christ will set up His millennial Kingdom, we read in 16:10, 11, "And the fifth angel poured out his vial upon the seat of the beast; and his kingdom was full of *darkness,* and they gnawed their tongues for pain, and blasphemed the God of heaven because of their pain and their sores and repented not of their deeds."

And again, Jude, in his brief letter, in showing the end of the apostasy, brings forth this argument (vv. 6, 13) "And the angels which kept not their first estate, but left their own habitation, he hath reserved in everlasting chains under *darkness* unto the judgment of the great day. . . . Raging waves of the sea, foaming out their own shame; wandering stars, to whom is reserved the blackness of *darkness* forever."

Besides the literal meaning, "darkness is frequently used in the Scriptures metaphorically. Since God is light, darkness is the natural antithesis of this. . . . the guiding 'pillar' was light to Israel but darkness to the Egyptians (Ex. 14:20),

and Sinai was covered with darkness when Jehovah descended
on it. (Ex. 20:21)."[19]

It might be noteworthy to mention here that the dispensation of the Law began in darkness, as mentioned above,
when God descended on Sinai, and it ended in darkness
with Christ hanging on the cross, becoming the final and
complete fulfillment of all that the Law demanded. Here
the Son of God, who, Himself, was and is the Light of the
world, bore the awfulness of the blackness and vileness of
sin and shame.

Darkness and judgment go together. Darkness signifies
judgment. "It was not a mere reaction of the natural sin,
but a sign that was wrought in the sun by God."[20]

MEANING OF THE DARKNESS

This leads us to consider the actual meaning of this darkness when Christ hung there on the cross. Truly, the darkness was a miracle. As all miracles in the Bible carry with
them a special teaching, we do well to consider some of
the things that this darkness portrays to us.

What a contrast between Bethlehem and Golgotha. The
natural man does not mind the Bethlehem story, the story
of the birth of Jesus, because it is full of light and cheer.
But the same natural man will shrink from Golgotha, because there he sees darkness, gloom, blood, and above all
else, he sees himself as he really is without God. Golgotha
is a revelation of man's hatred of God. Wilhelm Friedrich
Besser has well said, "On the fields of Bethlehem the Glory
of the Lord shone through the mid-night darkness to the
honor of the Christ.... On Golgotha it became dark at
bright noonday because the Light of the world sinks in
death ... and God sits in judgment."[21]

Could it be that the darkness was caused because the
Prince of darkness was permitted to exercise His power

---

[19] Hastings, *op cit.*, Vol. 1, page 559.
[20] Lenski, *op. cit.*, page 713.
[21] *The Passion Story*, page 287.

upon the Son of God for those three hours, Christ thus feeling to the fullest degree the impact of the wicked one? I would not want to state this dogmatically, but merely as a thought. Truly, as He was smitten of God, He was afflicted, and it seems that these afflictions came from another source rather than from the Father.

A. Lukyn Williams holds that nature was in sympathy with Christ: "When we consider what was being done on Calvary, who it was that was dying there, what was the object of His passion, what was the infinite and unspeakable effect of the sacrifice there offered, is it not wonderful that the Divine architect controlled nature to sympathize with her Creator, that as a supernatural effulgence heralded the Saviour's birth, a supernatural darkness should shroud His death?"[22] Yet, it seems to me that there was more involved than just sympathy on the part of the Father. The Father had completely forsaken the Son as He became the sin-bearer for all of mankind. Nothing was done to lighten the load or burden of sin as the Father "laid on him the iniquities of us all." He had forsaken the Son to such an extent that as Jesus was there on the cross and at the close of the three hours of darkness, He could not even call God, "Father," but simply cried out, "My God, my God, why hast thou forsaken me?" To say that the darkness was simply an indication of the sympathy on the part of the Father is to add sentimentality to the account that, it seems to me is not warranted by the teaching of the rest of the Scriptures.

The time that Christ was on the cross falls into three main periods, even as His years of ministry are divided into three periods. In His ministry there was the year of *inauguration,* which was followed by the year of *popularity,* and finally the year of *opposition.* There were also three periods at the crucifixion. There is some difference of opinion as to the exact order of events at the cross, but we are safe in saying that the first period was where Christ prayed for his enemies and took leave of His loved ones. In the second

---

[22] *Pulpit Commentary on Matthew,* Vol. 2, page 592.

period we have revealed to us man's hatred against Him.
And the third period is the period of *darkness,* where God's
hatred for sin is poured upon the innocent Sacrifice, Christ
Himself.

That which took place during those three hours when the
light in the sky failed was something so tremendous that
it cannot be described. Yet, "from heaven's standpoint, the
most tremendous period in all the running millenniums
were those three hours of darkness and silence."[23]

Besser says that this darkness typifies the night through
which Christ, the Crucified, was passing. Chrysostom says that
creation was unable to endure the shame to which its
Creator was being subjected by the creature.

> "Well might the sun in darkness hide,
> And shut His glories in,
> When Christ the mighty Maker died
> For man, the creature's sin."

In speaking of the awfulness of the death to which Christ
was subjected on our behalf, Edersheim wrote, "All nature
shrinks from death and there is a physical horror of the
separation between body and soul which, as purely natural
phenomenon, is in every instance only overcome, and that
only by a higher principle. And we conceive that the purer
the being the greater the violence of the tearing asunder
of the bond with which God Almighty originally bound
together body and soul. In the Perfect Man this must have
reached the highest degree. So also, He had in those dark
hours the sense of man-forsakenness and of His own isola-
tion from man; so, also had the intense silence of God,
the withdrawal of God, the sense of His God-forsakenness
and absolute loneliness. We dare not here speak of punitive
suffering but of forsakenness and loneliness. . . . Christ on
the cross suffered *for* man; He offered Himself a sacrifice;
He died for our sins, that, as death was the wages of sin,
so He died as the Representative of man — for man and in
the room of man."[24]

---

[23] G. Campbell Morgan, *The Gospel according to Matthew,* page 314.
[24] *Op. cit.,* Vol. 2, page 606.

We see the conflict that Christ went through concerning the approaching death there in the Garden of Gethsemane the night before His crucifixion. If it is true, as Edersheim says, "that the purer the being the greater the violence of the tearing asunder of the bond with which God Almighty originally bound together body and soul," how great must that experience have been for the holy, spotless Son of God. Truly the *darkness* is suitable to depict His awful death. From what Edersheim says in the above quote, he would have us to understand that the darkness speaks of the God-forsakenness Christ endured.

Through all this, there comes to us a wonderful truth which Besser brings to our attention. He says, "Yet the sun, though not visible for three hours, retained its light. Jesus, likewise, remained God's Son through those three hours, though His glory was not visible."[25] All the darkness and even His God-forsakenness did not do away with the *fact* of His Sonship.

"What Jesus suffered there for us and our salvation we cannot know, for during those three hours He hung upon His cross in silence and darkness; or if He spoke, there was none there to record His words. But toward the close of that time His anguish culminated and, emptied to the very uttermost of that glory which He had since the world began, — drinking to the very deepest dregs the cup of humiliation and bitterness, — enduring not only to have taken upon Him the form of a servant, but also to suffer the last infamy which human hatred could impose on servile helplessness — He uttered that mysterious cry, of which the full significance will never be fathomed by man, 'Eli, Eli, lama sabachthani?' "[26]

As Christ gave this cry, "some of them that stood there, when they heard that, said, This man calleth for Elias. . . . The rest said, Let be, let us see whether Elias will come to save him" (Matt. 27:47, 49). This seems to have been a wilful perversion of Christ's cry of distress and thus an added

25 *Op. cit.,* page 288.
26 Farrar, *op. cit.,* page 648.

insult. It is possible that those that stood around the cross during the darkness were mostly Roman soldiers and thus were not familiar with the Aramaic language which Christ employed when making this cry to God. Therefore, they might have thought that He was calling on one of the Jewish prophets. It is, however, more probable that the people wilfully misconstrued the cry of Christ and used it as another means of heaping more sorrow upon the Crucified.

Truly, we must say that He tasted to the fullest degree the awfulness of being lost and of enduring the death of separation from God. It is significant that the comfort which He had offered to the penitent thief just a short time before now had fled from Him. That brings our thoughts back again to the appalling darkness. "What He endured when He emptied the cup which He accepted in Gethsemane, He concealed from the eyes of man. Only eternity will fully reveal it and will cause the redeemed to sing praises to the Lamb."[27]

I feel justified in quoting Krummacher in several paragraphs to give us further light and food for thought concerning these three dark hours.

"Some have supposed it to convey a symbolical manifestation of the wrath of God against the murderers of Jesus. But such an interpretation is not in accordance with the event that is taking place on Calvary, and in which God, by the giving up of His only-begotten Son, evidences not merely His judicial severity and avenging justice, but especially His compassion for the murderers. The inference has also been drawn from the darkness that nature must have suffered in the death of Christ. But there seems little ground even for this explanation, since Christ, by His vicarious death, became, in an especial manner, the Renovator of nature.

"It has also been supposed that the nocturnal darkness typified the fact that with Christ, the light of the world was extinguished. But it was just in Christ's vicarious death that

---

27 Besser, *op. cit.,* page 288.

the Light of consolation and of real life rose upon the world. A sympathy also of the irrational creation with the pangs of its Lord and Master has been spoken of; but there is no room here for such poetic speculations. The sun did not obscure itself, but it was the Almighty who clothed it in the mourning-dress.

"The meaning is deeper.... But the chief object of the appalling phenomenon was to shadow forth by a stupendous figure, the mysterious position and inward state at the time, of Him who bled on the cross. The Lord withdrew Himself from the eyes of men behind the black curtain of appalling night, as behind the thick veil of the temple. He hung there full three hours on the cross, His thorn-crowned head drooping on His breast, involved in that darkness. He is in the Most Holy Place. He stands at the altar of the Lord. He performs His sacrificial function. He is the true Aaron, and at the same time the Lamb.

"That which, during this time, passed between Him and His Father, lies for the present sealed as with seven seals, hidden in the depth of eternity. We only know that behind the veil, He was engaged in the most ardent conflict, gained the most brilliant victory, and adorned His representative obedience with its final crown. We know that the grave of our sins was then dug; the handwriting that was against us taken out of the way; the curse which impended over us blotted out; and the wall which separated us from our God removed.

"Call the sight of the Redeemer weltering in His blood, and in total darkness, heartrending if you will; we know not a more delightful scene in heaven or on earth. The Man of the Cross is to us the fairest star in the horizon of the world. We behold it, and feel delivered from every evil. When Moses came forth from the darkness in which God dwelt, his face shone in such a manner that the astonished Israelites could not bear it.

"... The phenomenon signifies the withdrawing of another SUN than the earthly one — the obscuring of an inward world. It shadows the going down of a day of comfort and joy. Imagine to yourselves, if you can, a Man free from sin, holy, nay of divine nature, who calls the Almightly His light, God's nearness His paradise, and God's love His bliss. Imagine Him deprived of all this, no longer refreshed with any experience of the gracious presence of His heavenly Father, and although exclaiming, 'Whom have I in heaven but Thee?' banished into dreadful and horrifying visions of hell, and surrounded by nothing but images of sin and death. Imagine such a one, and then say if His state is not strikingly depicted by the midnight darkness which overspread the earth."[28]

The Gospel account has permitted us, to some degree, to observe the agony of Christ in Gethsemane. Peter, James and John were allowed to go with Jesus into the Garden. There was fought the greatest battle of the ages. But when the sufferings of Golgotha reached their zenith, God caused the darkness to cover the earth. God has never revealed what went on behind the curtain of darkness.

What Christ experienced on the cross, especially the last three hours, must be what He had in mind when He said, "I have a baptism to be baptized with; and how am I straitened till it be accomplished!" (Luke 12:50). However, as He looked beyond the cross and saw the outcome of this "baptism" of suffering, there was a certain joy even in the anticipation of the cross (Heb. 12:2). What could better portray the intenseness of His suffering than the blackness of midnight. The Baptism that Christ spoke of was that of being smitten not only of men, but also of God.

It was here that He experienced in reality what David cried out when he was fleeing for his life from his son Absalom, "Many there be which say of my soul, There is no help for him in God" (Ps. 3:2). David found help in God, and thus proved his accusers as false. But Jesus, while hanging on the cross, was so totally forsaken not only of His friends and disciples, but of God, that the cry of His heart, "My God, My God, why hast thou forsaken me?"

---

28 *The Suffering Saviour*, pages 379-381.

almost pierces through the pages to our ears today. It was the cry of a doomed soul.

This again reminds us of the prophetic words of David in the twenty-second Psalm, where we have the portrait of the suffering Saviour. This Psalm sets before us the three-fold suffering of Christ. We cannot do much more than just mention them here.

In verses 1 through 5 we have set before us the spiritual side of His sufferings. This was by far the greatest of His sufferings. As awful as His physical suffering was, it did not even begin to compare with the spiritual agony. It is possible that men at times have endured as much physical pain as Jesus did, but no one has ever tasted the awfulness of that suffering when the wrath of God against all the sin and wickedness of this world was poured forth upon Christ. No wonder we have the cry of verse 1, "My God, My God, *why* hast *thou* forsaken me?" In verses 4 and 5 he says, "Our fathers trusted in thee: they trusted and thou didst deliver them. They cried unto thee, and were delivered." Can you not feel the heartache at the thought that God heard the forefathers in their time of need, but now, His beloved Son, His only begotten Son could not get any help or comfort at all from the Father? Have you ever thought of how the Father felt when He could not reach down and help His Son out of the hands of the wicked? Oh, He could have, as far as ability was concerned, but He could not do it and also redeem lost mankind.

Beginning with verse 6 we have a clear description of the mental anguish of Jesus. He declared Himself to be but the off-cast of the earth, "I am a worm, and no man; a reproach of men, and despised of the people. All they that see me laugh me to scorn: they shoot out the lip, they shake the head, saying, He trusted on the Lord that he would deliver him: let him deliver him, seeing he delighted in him." (vv. 6-8). The fact of being put to open shame by the hostile crowd, and being mocked added to the sufferings. For He says, "They gaped upon me with their mouths, as a ravening and a roaring lion" (v. 13).

Beginning with verse 14, He speaks of the physical sufferings. He is here using terms that some mortal men might understand, having undergone physical sufferings themselves. He says, "I am poured out like water, and all my bones are out of joint: my heart is like wax; it is melted in the midst of my bowels. My strength is dried up like a potsherd; and my tongue cleaveth to my jaws; and thou hast brought me into the dust of death. . . . they pierced my hands and my feet. I may tell all my bones: they look and stare upon me" (vv. 14-17).

What better description can one find than that which we have just read to portray what Christ endured. The physical and mental anguish was His while the light was shining. But the spiritual torment is portrayed to us in the utter darkness. No better symbol could be employed to portray this than for the light of the sun to fail, causing total darkness.

We, as redeemed children of God who have been saved by believing that the death Christ died was our death, may in the sojourn of this life be called upon to enter into the fellowship of His sufferings, by enduring to some degree the mental and physical sufferings that He suffered. If we are deemed worthy to suffer for Him, let us count it all joy. But, blessed be His name, none of the redeemed will ever have to enter into that spiritual darkness of God-forsakenness that hung over Him and the earth those three awful, agonizing hours. "He was wounded for our transgressions, he was bruised for our iniquities: the chastisement of our peace *was upon him;* and with his stripes we are healed" (Isa. 53:5).

The darkness also speaks to us of the awfulness of the lost condition of those outside of Jesus Christ. How awful hell must be to make Christ willing to be "smitten of God" and become "sin for us," He "who knew no sin." The darkness shows to us the doom of the Christ-rejecting and neglecting sinner.

When we consider the sufferings of Christ for *all* of mankind (I John 2:2), no wonder the Bible says that those who

refuse to believe are "condemned already" (John 3:18), or
that "the wrath of God abideth on him" (John 3:36). The
same wrath that was poured forth upon the Son of God because of our sin will be poured upon those that will not
have by faith entered into a saving relationship with God
through the crucified Christ. The eternal punishment of the
lost is spoken of as "outer darkness" in the Gospel accounts
(Matt. 8:12; 22:13; 25:30).

The strongest argument for the reality of a literal hell,
aside from the clear statements of the Bible concerning it,
is "Golgotha." Why else, then, would the crucifixion have
been necessary? Aside from the fact of hell, Golgotha would
be a mockery.

The darkness of Golgotha symbolically speaks to us of
the awfulness and vileness of sin. It was while "Christ became sin for us" that the sky blackened. It was while God
judged sin that darkness enveloped the earth.

We have spoken of Christ being forsaken by the Father.
But why would God forsake His Son in such a crucial hour?
The only answer is found in that He, the Holy God, could
not look upon His Son as "He became sin for us." Sin must
be punished. Sin must be judged. God said, "The soul that
sinneth, it shall die" (Ezek. 18:20). Christ became sin, therefore He must die. That gives us an idea of what sin is to
God. Thus the darkness gives us an illustrative lesson on
the vileness and wickedness of the human heart.

How it must grieve the heart of our God as He looks
upon this sin-cursed earth and sees men walking about with
their hearts filled with every imagination of evil continually.
As natural men, we all stand before Him as sinners, for "all
have sinned and come short of the glory of God" (Rom.
3:21). "Behold, I was shapen in iniquity; and in sin did my
mother conceive me" (Ps. 51:5). Or, as the Prophet Isaiah
declared, "But we are *all* as an unclean thing, and all our
righteousnesses are as filthy [putrefying] rags" (Isa. 64:6).
Lo, if our righteousness, that is, the things we call good,
already is as filthy rags in the eyes of God, what must our
sins be like to Him. No wonder that, when Christ took

upon Himself all our sins, the wrath of God broke forth upon Him.

Darkness is an apt picture of our sins, for Paul says, "For ye were sometimes *darkness,* but now are ye light in the Lord" (Eph. 5:8). Again, He "hath delivered us from the power of darkness, and hath translated us into the kingdom of his dear Son" (Col. 1:13). How did He deliver us? By entering into the darkness for us, to bring us into His glorious kingdom of light. Thus, we as believers "are not in darkness, ... nor of darkness" (I Thess. 5:4, 5). It is declared of us that we have been "called out of darkness into his marvelous light" (I Peter 2:9). For us "the darkness is past, and the true light now shineth" (I John 2:8).

Though we were in darkness, and lived according to the course of this world, God took all of our sins, as vile as they were, "blotting out the handwriting of ordinances that was against us, which was contrary to us, and took it out of the way, *nailing it to his cross*" (Col. 2:14). Now, when God sees our sins, He sees them *on the cross.* The sin question has been settled. That is why we can say with utmost confidence, "There is therefore now *no* condemnation to them which are in Christ Jesus" (Rom. 8:1). But, oh, the price it cost the Father and the Son! Let us never rejoice in our salvation without remembering the *price* with which we have been bought.

Yes, "The struggle was long and hard, but from that hour when He died began the death-knell to every Satanic tyranny and every tolerated abomination. From that hour holiness became the universal ideal of all who name the name of Christ as their Lord."[29]

From the cross came that wonderful cry, "TETELESTAI" — "It is finished!" What is finished? The darkness with all of its implications is over. He has drunk the cup to the very last drop. The purpose for which He had come is finished. Not long before this He had said, "Even as the Son of man came not to be ministered unto, but to minister

---

[29] Farrar, *op. cit.,* page 652.

and to give his life a ransom for many" (Matt. 20:28). This was now accomplished. The Law had been fulfilled to the very letter; not "one jot or tittle" was left that was not fulfilled. Now the Father was free to receive all that would come to Him in the merits of that One who gave His life and blood there on the cross.

"TETELESTAI" was a cry of rejoicing that that hour for which He had come into the world was also over. The suffering which had consummated in the awful three hours of darkness and the experience of that God-forsakenness was now finished. He could now commit His spirit into the hands of the Father. He could again call God His Father.

What a victory! What a triumph has been wrought through the death of God's dear Son!

> "Alone upon the cross He hung That others He might save;
> Forsaken then by God and man, Alone, His life He gave."
> — Ben H. Price

> "Well might the sun in darkness hide,
> And shut his glories in,
> When Christ, the mighty Maker died
> For man the creature's sin."
> — Isaac Watts

2. The Rent Veil

The three hours of darkness had passed in almost complete silence. If anything was spoken by our Lord during that time, except the despairing cry, we know nothing about it. At the close of the darkness He cried, "I thirst" (John 19:28). This was definitely in fulfillment of the prophecy that declared, "In my thirst they gave me vinegar to drink" (Ps. 69:21). Upon receiving the drink, He declared, "It is finished" (John 19:30). One would think that by now all of His energy and strength would have ebbed away. But once again He cried, and this time not as one half dead but with a *loud voice,* "Father, into thy hands I commend my spirit" (Luke 23:46), after which "He gave up the ghost."

We must pause here in reverence. We see here the truth of the words spoken by our Lord during the days of his ministry, "No man taketh it [my life] from me, but I lay it down of myself" (John 10:18). He dismissed His Spirit. Thus the work for which He had come was completed.

As soon as He "yielded up the ghost," the "veil of the temple was rent in twain from the top to the bottom" (Matt. 27:51, Mark 15:38, Luke 23:45). What a sight! With the passing of darkness, there came that clear ringing voice declaring the committal of His Spirit into the hands of the Father. Then and there the veil of the temple tore from the top to the bottom, the earth quaked, the rocks rent and the graves were opened. Though God did not interfere with the crucifixion, after the atonement was completed He spoke through these sudden occurrences. No wonder then that "the people that came together to that sight, beholding the things which were done, smote their breasts" (Luke 23:48).

WHEN DID THE VEIL REND IN TWAIN?

In studying the second miracle in connection with the death of Jesus, we would do well to establish in our minds the time *when* the veil was rent.

"The rending of the veil is mentioned by the synoptics as consequent on, and occurring simultaneously with, the completion of the ineffable sacrifice."[1] How significant that the rending of the veil should occur just when Jesus' life expired, and that at the time the priests were to offer the evening sacrifice in the temple. To this agree a number of Bible scholars, as we will see a little later. Be it sufficient at this time to give just one quotation. "As we compute, it may just have been the time when at the evening sacrifice, the officiating priesthood entered the Holy Place, either to burn incense or to do other service there."[2]

QUOTATIONS FROM ANCIENT WRITERS

While considering the time of the occurrence of the rending of the veil, I would refer to some of the ancient records which state the fact that something out of the ordinary did happen in the temple on the day of the Passover, the day Jesus died. I will quote just a few men who are considered authorities.

"Jewish tradition plainly points to noticeable events in the temple, when it relates that, forty years before the destruction of the temple, the light on the golden candlestick was extinguished, the gate of the temple flew open at night time of its own accord."[3]

"In the *Gemara* it is stated that some forty years before the destruction of Jerusalem, the heavy gates of the temple, which could with difficulty be moved by *many* men, and which were locked at the time, flew open about midnight at the Passover. Josephus (B. J. vi. 5.3) reports an occur-

---

[1] *Pulpit Commentary on Matthew,* Vol. 2, page 294.
[2] Edersheim, *op. cit.,* page 611.
[3] J. P. Lange, *The Life of the Lord Jesus Christ,* Vol. 3 of the Gospels, page 323.

rence of this kind shortly before the capture of the city. As Neander remarks, these accounts hint as *some* strange occurrence being remembered in connection with the time of the crucifixion."[4]

"That some great catastrophe, betokening the impending destruction of the temple, had occurred in the Sanctuary about this very time, is confirmed by not less than four mutually independent testimonies: those of Tacitus (Hist. v. 13), of Josephus (*Jew. War* vl. 5.3), of the *Talmud* (Jer. Yoma 43c; Yoma 39b), and of earliest Christian tradition. ... The most important of these are, of course, the *Talmud* and the writings of Josephus. The latter speaks of the mysterious extinction of the middle and chief light in the Golden Candlestick, forty years before the destruction of the Temple; and both he and the *Talmud* refer to a supernatural opening by themselves of the great temple-gate that had been previously closed, which was regarded as a portent of the coming destruction of the Temple. We can scarcely doubt that some historical fact must underlie so peculiar and widespread a tradition, and we cannot help feeling that it may be a distorted version of the occurrence of the rending of the temple veil at the crucifixion of Christ."[5]

With the threefold testimony of the synoptic Gospel writers along with these historical records, it is quite conclusive that the rending of the veil took place together with the death of Christ, and that it was widely known. It was not something that was done in secret, even though it was not as public as the other sign-miracles.

WHICH VEIL WAS RENT?

With the declaration of the rending of the veil, there arises in our minds the question as to which veil it was that was rent in two, because there were at least two veils or curtains in the temple in Jerusalem.

---

[4] From a footnote in *The International Critical Commentary* on Luke, p. 538.
[5] Edersheim, *op. cit.*, page 610.

The Gospel accounts declare that it was "the veil [or curtain] of the Sanctuary (TO KATAPETASMA TOU NAOU)." The NAOS was the shrine of the temple, the Holy of Holies, which was the place where God dwelt symbolically, was divided from the Holy place (HIERON) of the temple with a thick veil called KATAPETASMA. There was another veil that divided the Holy place from the porch or outer court, which was called KALUMMA. The Synoptics expressly say that it was the KATAPETASMA that was rent from top to bottom. "The rending of the veil is mentioned by the Synoptics as consequent on, and occurring simultaneously with, the completion of the ineffable sacrifice. . . . This was the veil between the Holy place and the Holy of Holies."[6]

DESCRIPTION OF THE VEIL

The specifications for the veil in the Tabernacle are given in Exodus 26:31-35. "And thou shalt make a veil of blue, and purple, and scarlet, and fine twined linen of cunning work: with cherubims shall it be made: and thou shalt hang it upon four pillars of shittim wood overlaid with gold: their hooks shall be of gold, upon the four sockets of silver. And thou shalt hang up the veil under the taches, that thou mayest bring in thither within the veil the ark of the testimony: and the veil shall divide *unto you* between the holy place and the most holy. And thou shalt put the mercy seat upon the ark of the testimony in the most holy place. And thou shalt set the table without the veil, and the candlestick over against the table on the side of the tabernacle toward the south: and thou shalt put the table on the north side."

The Holy place and the Holy of Holies in the Temple were reconstructed according to the pattern of the Tabernacle. Though the veil in the Temple was much larger than the one in the Tabernacle, it served the same purpose. We learn that the veil was "large and costly, some sixty feet high and made of rich materials. Josephus (*Bell. Jud.* v. 5.4)

---

[6] *Pulpit Commentary* on Matthew, Vol. 2, page 594.

tells us of one of the veils in the temple, that it was a Babylonian curtain, embroidered with linen in various colors, woven together with wonderful art, such as the eye loved to rest upon."[7]

An interesting account concerning the temple veil is found in the following quotation: "According to an account dating from Temple-times, . . . the veil before the Most Holy place was 40 cubits [60 feet] long, and 20 cubits [30 feet] wide, of the thickness of the palm of the hand, and wrought in 72 squares, which were joined together; and this veil was so heavy, that in the exaggerated language of the time, it needed 300 priests to manipulate it."[8]

We saw in Exodus 26:31 that the veil was made of fine-twined linen, and that the colors were blue, purple and scarlet. It was embroidered with cherubim. When the temple was constructed, the same pattern was followed by Solomon. It is quite evident that this same pattern was followed in Herod's temple which stood in the day of Christ.

Ferdinand Prat, in a footnote indicates that an ancient writer, Mishuah, agrees with the general dimensions and description given by Edersheim.[9] It was this veil that rent in two at the time of Christ's death.

A GLIMPSE BEHIND THE VEIL

According to historical records, it was not only the officiating priests at this particular time that would see the rent veil, but other priests as well. Possibly, also, some of the people standing outside on the porch would see it, as "it was the duty of the officiating priests, on the evening of the day of preparation, at the hour of evening prayer, which would correspond to the time of the Lord's death, to enter into the Holy place, where he would of course be between the two curtains, or veils, the outer veil and the inner veil. It would then be his business to roll back the KALUMMA, or *outer veil,* thus exposing the Holy place to the people, who

---

[7] *Ibid.,* page 594.
[8] Edersheim, *op. cit.,* page 610.
[9] Prat, *op. cit.,* page 397.

would be in the outer court. And then and there they would
see, to the amazement of all, the KATAPETASMA, the
inner veil, rent asunder from top to bottom."[10]

In this connection, Edersheim raises a very interesting
question, "May this phenomenon account for the early con-
version of so many priests?"[11] We read concerning the work
of the early church that "the word of God increased; and
the number of the disciples multiplied in Jerusalem, and
a great company of the *priests* were obedient to the faith"
(Acts 6:7).

The idea that the rending of the veil occurred at the
time when the priests were offering the evening oblation
has caused some to be "carried away" in the use of their
imagination. For example, Krummacher, in his fine devotional work entitled, *The Suffering Saviour,* makes this mistake,
He says, "The priests begin their customary duties, when
at the very moment in which Christ on Calvary exclaimed,
'Father, into thy hands I commit my spirit!' Who can
describe the astonishment of the sons of Aaron! The thickly-
woven, heavy veil, without being touched by any human
hand, is rent in twain, in the midst, from top to the bottom,
and *the mercy-seat with the ark of the covenant and the
golden cherubim,* that sacred depository which the high
priest alone was permitted to approach, not without blood,
and only once a year, *stands suddenly naked and unveiled*
to the view of everyone."[12] All of this would be true *if* the
ark of the covenant and the golden cherubim had still been
behind the veil. But historical records indicate that "the
Holy of Holies was empty; only a stone was in the temple
of Zerubbabel, on which the high priest placed his censer
on the day of atonement."[13] The Holy of Holies was empty
because the "ark of the covenant was destroyed in the destruction of Jerusalem by Nebuchadnezzar."[14] To this agrees

10 *Pulpit Commentary* on Mark, Vol. 2, page 309.
11 *Op. cit.,* Vol. 2, page 611.
12 Page 411.
13 *International Standard Bible Encyclopedia,* Vol. 5, page 2938.
14 *Ibid.,* Vol. 1, page 245.

Lenski, for he says, "In Herod's sanctuary, the Holy of Holies was empty, for the ark of the covenant that had stood there in Solomon's temple had been destroyed."[15]

Since there is no evidence anywhere that the ark of the covenant had been reconstructed, it is quite evident that all that the priests saw when the veil was rent was an empty room, which had been filled with darkness.

WHAT CAUSED THE VEIL TO BE RENT?

The direct cause of the rending of the veil is discussed with various opinions among writers. Some think that the earthquake caused the veil to be rent in twain. Yet others believe that is was the direct work of God, apart from the earthquake. "According to Jerome, the *Gospel of the Hebrews* related that an immense beam of the temple did fall down. If we suppose, then, that such a beam fell athwart the covering veil, we have suggested to us the possibility of the rent occurring from the top to the bottom."[16] Furthermore, we read that "while the rending of the veil is recorded first, as being the most significant token to Israel, it may have been connected with the earthquake, although this alone might scarcely account for the tearing of so heavy a veil from top to bottom."[17]

That the rent in the veil was due to an earthquake seems unlikely, as there were other veils, and only this one is mentioned as rent. Also, there is no further indication that the Temple was damaged by the earthquake. If the rent was caused by an earthquake, certainly there would be record of damage to the Temple sufficient to warrant such a rent in so heavy and strong a veil. "If the veil was at all such as described in the *Talmud,* it could not have been rent in twain by a mere earthquake or the fall of the lintel. One would think that they all understood that it meant that God's own hand had rent the veil and forever deserted

---

15 *Op. cit.,* page 724.
16 Lange, *op. cit.,* page 327.
17 Edersheim, *op. cit.,* page 610.

the Most Holy place where He had so long dwelt in the mysterious gloom."[18]

It is also significant that the Gospel account expressly mentions the rending of the veil before the earthquake and the other accompanying signs, as if to make sure that the rending would not be attributed to the convulsion in the earth. The Holy Spirit makes no mistakes in the choice of words or arrangements of incidents.

Lenski declares, "We have no intimation that it was caused by the earthquake.... Then it would indeed not have split from the top down to the very bottom, but would have been torn in several directions. The idea that it was fastened to a great beam at the top and that this beam broke in two, and thus tore the curtain, is an improvable supposition."[19]

Evidence is lacking in proving that the rent in the inner veil was caused by the earthquake. The strongest indications are that the veil rent independently of the earthquake, though the occurrence may have been almost or altogether simultaneously. The rent was caused by the hand of God. It was a divine act. It was nothing less than a *sign miracle*.

The mind of unbelief and liberal thought has by no means overlooked this portion of Biblical teaching. Here, too, the doubters doubt and the unbelievers do not believe, as shown in the following brief quotation: "It seems quite likely that some of these portents [the rending of the veil and earthquake] found their way into the narrative for symbolic value, rather than as reports of actual happenings."[20] If these occurrences are just recorded for symbolic value rather than for true facts, there is then no value in them for us. If the veil did not actually rend in two, our faith in its teaching is vain.

THE MEANING OF THE VEIL

The veil, we saw before, separated the Holy of Holies from the Holy place. This indicated that heaven and God were

---

18 *Ibid.*, page 611.
19 *Op. cit.*, page 724.
20 *The Interpreter's Bible*, Vol. 7, page 907.

inaccessible to all until Christ, by His death, rent the veil in twain and opened the way into the true presence of God, of which the Holy of Holies was but a symbol. The veil taught that access to God was closed.

Throughout the years they had worshipped before the veil, none daring to enter behind the veil, except the appointed high priest, once a year on the Day of Atonement. The Lord indicated by the veil "that the way into the Holiest of all was not yet manifest" (Heb. 9:8), or that the way was simply closed. All of those years no mortal man dared to approach God nor to enter where the cherubim bowed in worship over the mercy seat. Only once every year, on the appointed Day of Atonement, the high priest entered through the veil, where he first offered blood for the remission of his own sins, and then for the sins of the people (Heb. 9:7, Lev. 16:14).

As the high priest entered behind the veil with the censer and the blood for the atonement of the people's sins, the Israelites would stand outside, waiting for him to return. Those were anxious moments. The atonement for their sins depended upon the acceptance of the high priest and the offering he brought to God. If he came with a sacrifice that was not acceptable, or if he came, himself, in a way not acceptable to God, the high priest would be struck dead, and their sins would remain uncovered. But the moment the high priest returned from behind the veil, they rested assured that the atonement had been accepted. What rejoicing came to their hearts when the high priest appeared again from behind the veil, for now they, too, stood accepted before God until one day God would send the true Sacrifice to atone for their sins. Thus Jesus, our High Priest, with His own blood entered once into God's presence, removing the veil that separated us from God. Now, for those who come to God by Christ, He is able to save by virtue of the blood that was shed, and furthermore, give free and personal access to His own glorious presence.

Referring again to the account in Leviticus 16, where the high priest entered once a year into God's presence, it

signified "that *access for sinners* to a Holy God is only
through atoning blood. But, as they had only the blood of
bulls and goats which could not take away sin (Heb. 10:4),
during all the long ages that preceded the death of Christ,
the thick veil remained. The blood of bulls and goats continued to be shed and sprinkled; and once a year access to
God through an atoning sacrifice was vouchsafed — *in a
picture,* or rather was *dramatically presented,* in those symbolical actions — nothing more. But NOW, the one atoning
sacrifice being provided in the precious blood of Christ,
access to this holy God could no longer be denied; and so
the moment the victim expired on the altar [cross], that
thick veil which for so many ages had been the dreaded
symbol of *separation between God and guilty man* was,
without a hand touching it, mysteriously rent in twain from
top to bottom."[21] The door and the throne of God, no
longer just the mercy seat, opened wide to all who desire to
come. And we can come, not as a beggar but boldly to Him,
"Who through the eternal spirit offered himself without
spot to God" (Heb. 9:14). There was a time when it was
death to go in to the presence of God; now it is *death to
stay out.* It is because Jesus entered once into the presence
of God the Father with His own blood that this dark veil
has now been removed, not only from between us and God's
presence, but also from our hearts. By virtue of the death
of Jesus Christ, God is "able to save to the uttermost all
that come unto God by him" (Heb. 7:25).

Thus it is that through His death, we have "boldness to
enter into the holiest by the blood of Jesus, by a new and
living way, which he hath consecrated for us, through the
veil, that is to say, his flesh" (Heb. 10:20). The rending
of the veil thus indicated the opening of, and access to,
Heaven through the wounded body of the Son of God.

By His death, when the veil was rent, access to the Father
was opened to all men. The division that was between the

---

[21] Jamieson, Fausset and Brown, *A Commentary, Critical, Experimental
and Practical,* Vol. 5, page 128.

priest and the worshipper is now gone. The church has now
entered into the position of the priesthood (I Peter 2:9).
All have access to God through Jesus Christ.

SYMBOLIC WORSHIP ENDED

The writer of the Epistle to the Hebrews, in dealing with
our new access to God by the way of the Crucified One,
declared, "Having therefore, brethren, boldness to enter into the holiest by the blood of Jesus, by a new and living
way, which he hath consecrated for us, through the veil,
that is to say, his flesh; and having an high priest over the
house of God; let us draw near with a true heart in full
assurance of faith, having our hearts sprinkled from an evil
conscience, and our bodies washed with pure water" (Heb.
10:19-22).

What do we have in Christ? We have boldness. The same
writer said, "Let us come boldly unto the throne of grace"
(Heb. 4:16). During the days of the Old Testament Law,
men came with fear lest their sacrifice be not accepted. They
came, not with full assurance and boldness, but as though
walking on uncertain ground. Why then can we come boldly?
Because the acceptable sacrifice for us has been offered in
the death of Jesus Christ. How do we know that this sacrifice is acceptable to God? God declared the same by the
miraculous signs that accompained Christ's death. Of special
significance to us is the rending of the veil.

We now come boldly because we come to God in the
merit of the sacrifice He has already accepted. When we
come *in the name of Jesus Christ,* we are received *in His
name.* We have boldness because the blood sacrifice which
we claim as the ground of our righteousness is the blood of
the Holy Son of God. To reject us when we come *in His
name* would be for Him to reject His own Son.

There is a definite connection between the rending of the
veil and the function of the temple worship. The worship
in the temple had significance up to the time of Christ's
death, the people being commanded to worship by use of

symbols. But the death of Christ ended all symbol worship. The symbols have lost their significance in the fulfillment of Christ, their antitype. "The rending of the veil perhaps symbolized the *end* of the temple and its service."[22] This fact seems to be emphasized by the accompanying signs in the temple that were referred to by ancient writers, which we mentioned earlier. That, in reality, is also the reason why God permitted the temple to be destroyed in A.D. 70. The true function of the temple had ended. The rending of the veil declared that God no longer is to be localized but worship is now universal, and that "the whole of the Jewish dispensation, with its rites and ceremonies, was now unfolded by Christ: and that thenceforth the middle wall of partition was broken down so that now, not Jew only, but the Gentile also might draw nigh by the blood of Christ."[23]

The Holy of Holies was the shadow and type of the throne-room of Heaven (Heb. 8:1-6). But the rent veil now declares that we have access to God, not on the merits of our own goodness but on the merit of Christ. Thus, all believers have become a kingdom of priests, with the right of free access to God at all times. The minister is not officially nearer to God than the so-called layman. Each must and can come for himself. All that come the new and living way are accepted. It is a *living* way because He is the *life-giving* Saviour.

Morgan, in this connection, says, "That was a great symbolic act, indicating the fact that the symbolism was forever over."[24] Again, Lange declares, "When, in so momentous an hour, in an extraordinary manner, the curtain which veiled the Holy of Holies was rent, this must appear to the believing mind as a sign from God that the God-worship of the temple was abrogated and for the time to come rejected by Jehovah."[25]

22 Plummer, *op. cit.*, page 538.
23 *Pulpit Commentary on Mark*, Vol. 2, page 309.
24 *Op. cit.*, page 315.
25 *Op. cit.*, page 323.

LAW FULFILLED

The rent veil would indicate that Christ had, in His death, fulfilled to the very letter every demand of the Law. It is because of this fulfillment that Temple worship by symbol lost its significance. Now, worship is to be "in spirit and in truth, for the Father seeketh such to worship him" (John 4:23). We no longer need the symbols because we worship in faith. We now have the *reality* in the resurrected Christ, through whom we now come to the Father. The work of the high priest of the old order is ended and the great sacrifice by the High Priest, Jesus Christ has been offered, and He now is in the *true* Holy of Holies. "For Christ is not entered into the holy places made with hands, ... but into heaven itself, now to appear in the presence of God for us" (Heb. 9:24).

Thus, we want to emphasize that the rending of the veil was a "renewed intimation that the Levitical service, though divinely ordered and prophetically significant, contained only types of a coming salvation, which, now that the latter was accomplished, were rendered void, even as the blossom is expelled by the fruit."[26]

FEAR OF DEATH REMOVED

It would appear that the veil in the temple is representative of another veil, that is, the terrible veil of the fear of death. This veil, too, was rent in twain by the death of Christ. For through the sacrificial death of Christ, the suffering of death and of judgment which had until then terrified humanity, was put away by the One Great Sacrifice. He took the sting of death upon Himself. The "stinger" has been removed from death. Now, by faith, we can look beyond the grave and say, "O death, where is thy sting? O grave, where is thy victory" (I Cor. 15:55).

---

[26] Krummacher, *op. cit.*, page 411.

ACCESS TO GOD OPENED

As long as the veil remained, the presence of God to the mind of the Jew was a mystery. That is, He dwelt symbolically in the gloom and darkness behind the veil. God was unapproachable. Truly, under such circumstances, they could not have come with real joy to worship. They could not help realizing, when they looked at the temple with the veil, that they were shut out from the presence of God. Their approach to Him was dependent upon the fitness of the high priest who would be ministering on their behalf. The veil thus excluded men from God. Morgan says, concerning this, "Think of the Holy of Holies in the temple of Jerusalem, *of its darkness!* No light was ever there! There had been light in the olden days when the glory of the *Shekinah* shone between the overshadowing wings of the cherubim; but that had long since passed away. Men were outside, not permitted to enter. But when the King died, the veil was rent, and that meant first that light broke through where all had been darkness, and secondly, that God, Who had been a mystery, became a Revelation, shining out upon all human history; and it meant also that excluded men were admitted. What happened when the veil was rent? All the world was brought inside; and all souls were made priests, who come through the name and merit of the Priest Who that day had died."[27] Thus, through Christ, the veil between God and man was removed by the effectual sacrifice which rent the veil in two. So it is that when we place our faith in the finished work of Christ, the blindness that is upon the spiritual eyes of all natural men is removed, and we enter into full fellowship with God. We have access to God.

We have repeatedly stated that the veil indicated the separation that existed between God and man. Let us remember, however, that it was not the plan and will of God that this separation should be. Man, the crown of God's creation, had been created for fellowship with God. That

[27] *Op. cit.,* page 315.

was God's purpose and intention for man. This is seen in His fellowship with Adam and Eve in the Garden of Eden. But because of the disobedience of the first parents, a wedge or separation came between God and man which was symbolized by the veil.

The evidence that it was not in the plan of God to have the veil between Himself and man is seen in the temporary provision of access to Himself as given in the Old Testament and then the permanent access through the sacrifice of His only begotten Son, offered to open the way into His presence. It is also evident in that man is not *right* socially, morally, or spiritually until he is brought back into fellowship with God through the new birth, by receiving this sacrifice of Christ on Golgotha.

Thus, we must say that the veil, which separated man from God, is man's sinful flesh. The Psalmist cried, "Who shall ascend unto the hill of the Lord, and who shall stand in his holy place?" The answer he gave is, "he that hath clean hands and a pure heart, who hath not lifted up his soul unto vanity" (Ps 24:3, 4). But, as Krummacher said, "Who could boast of being thus blameless in the sight of God? There is none righteous, no not one.... But what remains for anyone, except the mournful ejaculation of the prophet, 'woe is me, for I am undone, for I am a man of unclean lips!' Righteousness had departed; sin reigned."[28] Thus, the veil of our sinful self and flesh stood between us and God. It was not a barrier constructed by God, but by man's sinfulness.

But once more God took the first step to prepare a way to break down the awful veil. Again, using the temple veil as the picture of that veil of sinful flesh between us and God, He broke every fetter that thus separated us. His Son tasted death for every man during those hours on the cross. He publicly manifested that now this veil was done away in Christ. Let me quote Krummacher again, "Suddenly the sign in the temple announces that our position as regards

---

[28] *Op. cit.*, page 411, 412.

the habitation of the Most High, had undergone a great and thorough change. That which hindered our access to the sanctuary of God was done away. That which elevated itself as a wall of separation between us and Him fell down. There is no longer any risk in casting ourselves into the hands of Him before whom even angels are not pure. Put on the Lord Jesus Christ and then thou mayest boldly and with childlike confidence enter the Father's holy habitation which henceforward stands open to thee day and night.... The Saviour, by His death, threw open every door and gate into heaven."[29]

That is why it was necessary for the Son of God to take upon Himself the form of man. "Forasmuch then, as the children are partakers of flesh and blood, he also Himself likewise took part of the same; that through death he might destroy him that had the power of death, that is, the devil" (Heb. 2:14). He took upon Himself human flesh that He might prepare the way into the presence of the Father through the rent veil. The rent veil was the broken body, representing the sinful flesh of all mankind. "By this act of mediation, He answered and fulfilled everything requisite for our justification in the sight of God, and therefore, also for our admission before the throne of God."[30]

Thus, we see that our salvation from start to finish is all by the grace of God, and "not of works, lest any man should boast" (Eph. 2:9).

> "There was no other good enough,
>   To pay the price of sin;
>   He only could unlock the gate
>   Of heaven and let us in."
>   — Cecil F. Alexander

---

[29] *Ibid.*, page 412.
[30] *Ibid.*, page 413.

3. The Earth Quaked, Rocks Rent and Graves Opened

"And behold the veil of the temple was rent in twain from the top to the bottom; and the earth did quake, and the rocks rent; and the graves were opened" (Matt. 27:51, 52a).

This occurrence is another one of the miraculous events that took place in connection with the crucifixion of Christ. After the three hours of unusual darkness in midday, when the Lord had completed the sacrifice for sin on the cross, He committed His Spirit into the hands of the loving Father, who had just previously found it necessary to forsake the Son. With the shout of triumph from the lips of the crucified, the veil of the temple was rent in twain, the earth did quake, the rocks rent and graves were opened. The events that followed His death were symbols of *victory,* not defeat. Even the final cry of Christ on the cross was one of *victory.*

In this section we are going to deal with the earthquake and the direct results of it.

This miracle is *one.* Although Bishop Nicholson deals with it as two different miracles, the Bible, I believe, treats it as *one.* We shall see that there are different spiritual lessons in this, but as far as the occurrence is concerned, it is all hinged upon this one fact — the earth quaked, which produced a two-fold result. Because we are dealing with the miracles that occurred, we want to include this entire miracle in this one chapter.

Basically, the whole occurrence is for the purpose of showing forth the reality of Christ's Messiahship.

The rending of the rocks was the earth's response to the redemption wrought by Christ. Christ came as King, not only of a heavenly kingdom, but also of an earthly kingdom. Matthew, in his account of the Gospel, set forth Christ as the Messiah. This was his main theme. In fact, the Gospel according to Matthew is frequently called the Gospel of the Kingdom, setting forth Christ as the long-looked-for Messiah. It is significant that Matthew is the only one of the Gospel writers that mentioned anything about the earthquake at the time of the Redeemer's death.

So, at the time that He dismissed (literally, *sent away*) His Spirit, God caused a "miraculous convulsion of the earth in attestation of the truth that the Sufferer was the Messiah, the Son of God...."[1] Basically, the whole event has one fundamental lesson. It is to set forth the fact that Jesus truly was the Messiah, even as He had claimed to be. This is borne out by the testimony of the Roman soldiers: "Now, when the centurion, and they that were with him, watching Jesus, saw the earthquake, and those things that were done, they feared greatly, saying, Truly this was the Son of God" (Matt. 27:54). Though Mark and Luke do not record this event, itself, they do record the testimony of the centurion (Mark 15:39, Luke 23:47) which would presuppose some miraculous event, such as Matthew here records.

EXTENT OF THE QUAKE

There is nothing in the Gospel records that definitely tells us how far the earthquake extended. It simply states that "the earth did quake." The extent of it is not stated as specifically as is the extent of the darkness, of which it says, "there was darkness over all the land," or "over all the earth." William R. Nicholson thinks that it was the immediate area of Calvary where the concussion was felt, at the very place of crucifixion.[2] Another feels that "from what

---

[1] Albert Barnes, *Barnes' Notes on the New Testament,* on Matthew and Mark, page 313.

[2] *The Six Miracles on Calvary,* page 55.

follows, it would seem that this earthquake was local, having for its object the rending of the rocks and opening of
the graves."[3] Still another writer declared that "there was a
local earthquake at this awful moment."[4] But Albert Barnes
states, "It was not confined to Judea, but was felt in other
countries. It is mentioned by Roman writers."[5] It is regret-
able that he does not state his authority for that statement.
I have been able to find just one reference regarding the
extent of the earthquake going beyond Judea, by an ancient
writer. This one was written by a Greek writer, and the
quotation follows: "Arnobius (in adv *Gentes,* I.53) says
that all the elements of the universe were thrown into con-
fusion; and in the writings attributed to Dionysius the
Areopagite it is said that, when the philosophers at Athens
could not explain these wonders, it was concluded that the
God of nature was suffering, and the people raised an altar
to Him with the inscription, TO THE UNKNOWN GOD."[6]
There is no way of tracing the accuracy of this statement,
but if it is reliable, as Plummer seems to indicate, it is interesting to note that the Greeks attributed the altar "to
the unknown god" to the miracles that attended the death
of Jesus. Could that be the reason why Paul said to the
Athenians, "Whom therefore ye ignorantly worship, *him
declare I unto you*" (Acts 17:23)?

The authority of the above quotation cannot be checked,
but there seems to be some indication that the convulsion
was felt beyond the immediate area of Judea.

Though the burden of proof for the earthquake, with the
accompanying results at the time of Christ's death, rests upon
the records of Matthew's Gospel account, we do well to see
what some of the ancient and also the contemporary writers
have to say concerning evidences of the earthquake at Jerusalem.

---

[3] Jamieson, Fausset and Brown, *op. cit.,* page 127.
[4] *Pulpit Commentary,* Vol. 2 on Matthew, page 549.
[5] *Op. cit.,* page 313.
[6] From a footnote in *An Exegetical Commentary on the Gospel According to St. Matthew,* page 402.

SIGNS AT JERUSALEM

Travelers through the area of Jerusalem have been greatly impressed with the "extraordinary rents and fissures that have been observed in the rocks near this spot."[7] Further, "The fact of the earthquake is testified by Phlegon, whose words were quoted by Julius Africanus in his *Chronographis,* and by Eusebius in his *Chronicon* (the passage no longer extant in the original, being preserved by Jerome, and in an American version). The rending of the rocks is attested by St. Cyril, Bishop of Jerusalem (*Catches.* XIII.33), who speaks of remarkable fissures in Golgotha, which he had often noticed."[8] Barnes comments that "rocks are still seen at Mount Calvary thus rent asunder, which are *said* to be the ones that were convulsed when the Saviour died."[9] Here, again, let me say that these quotations do not prove anything, but rather they confirm what the Bible already declares.

An earthquake in the general area of Jerusalem was, in reality, nothing unusual. In fact, that part of the world is just about as much in an earthquake zone as is the west coast of the United States. This was illustrated in a recent geological "earthquake map" of the world.

EARTHQUAKES REFERRED TO IN SCRIPTURE

Earthquakes have their place in the records of the Bible, in history as well as in prophecy. In Christ's Olivet discourse, He said, "For nation shall rise against nation, and kingdom against kingdom: and there shall be famines, and pestilences, and *earthquakes,* in divers places" (Matt. 24:7). When the sixth seal shall be opened in heaven, according to the Apocalypse, it says, "and, lo, there was a great *earthquake*" (Rev. 6:12). In the scene of the angels before the altar, it says, "And the angel took the censer and filled it with fire of the altar, and cast it into the earth: and there were voices, and thunderings, and lightings, and an *earthquake*" (Rev. 8:5).

---

[7] Jamieson, Fausset and Brown, *op. cit.,* page 127.
[8] *Pulpit Commentary,* Vol. 2 on Matthew, page 596.
[9] *Op. cit.,* page 314.

In announcing the second woe in Rev. 11:13, we read, "And the same hour was there a great *earthquake*, and the tenth part of the city fell, and in the *earthquake* were slain seven thousand: and the remnant were affrighted, and gave glory to the God of heaven." In speaking of the seventh vial of the wrath of God, we read, "And there were voices, and thunders and lightnings; and there was a great *earthquake*, such as was not since men were upon the earth, so mighty an *earthquake*, and so great" (Rev. 16:18). In these verses we see that earthquakes are to have a prominent part in the judgment on the earth just prior to and during the tribulation period.

There was the earthquake at Mount Sinai at the giving of the Law. We shall refer to this again just a little later when we shall seek to find the true meaning of Golgotha's quake. Moreover, while the children of Israel were in the wilderness during the time of Korah's rebellion against the leadership of Moses and Aaron, God caused the earth to rend apart and swallow up Korah and his followers (Numbers 16:31).

These earthquakes seem to be judgments of God upon the ungodly for their rebellion against the Son of God. But the earthquake at the time of the death of Christ was one of triumph, and a token of *victory*. It was a symbol of joy rather than of vengeance. Through the death of Christ the demands of the law were met, and now God could be "just and the justifier of him that believeth in Jesus" (Rom. 3:26).

In His sermon on the Mount, Jesus declared, "Think not that I am come to destroy the law, or the prophets: I am not come to destroy, but to fulfil" (Matt. 5:17). Christ, in His life and death, perfectly fulfilled every demand of the Law. He was everything the prophets had foretold. There was not one of the prophecies that was not completed in Christ. He was born of Jewish ancestry, under the Law. He lived a life completely without sin. He never once sinned in thought, desire or deed. He could turn to the accusers and say, "Which of you convinceth me of sin?" (John 8:46). Of Him Peter could say, "Who did no sin, neither was guile found in his mouth" (I Peter 2:22). Of Him we read, that

He "was in all points tempted like as we are, yet without sin" (Heb. 4:15). Just as the *type* had to be without blemish (28 times we read in Leviticus that the sacrifice must be "without blemish"), even so Christ was declared the "lamb without blemish and without spot" (I Peter 1:19). In this He perfectly fulfilled the requirements of the Law.

It was not only in His life that He fulfilled the demands of the Law, but much more so in His death. We read in the Biblical commentary to the book of Leviticus, namely Hebrews, thus: "But Christ being come an high priest of good things to come, by a greater and more perfect tabernacle, not made with hands, that is to say, not of this building; neither by the blood of goats and calves, but by his own blood he entered in once into the holy place, having obtained eternal redemption for us. For if the blood of bulls and of goats, and the ashes of an heifer sprinkling the unclean, sanctifieth to the purifying of the flesh: How much more shall the blood of Christ, who through the eternal Spirit offered himself without spot to God, purge your conscience from dead works to serve the living God? . . . but now once in the end of the world hath he appeared to put away sin by the sacrifice of himself" (Heb. 9:11-14, 26). Thus, in His death, He fulfilled every requirement of the Law. He accomplished all that He set out to do.

THE EARTHQUAKE AT MOUNT SINAI

In the light of this, let us go back to another earthquake, a quake which shook Mount Sinai with such intensity that the children of Israel feared greatly, and requested that from henceforth God should speak to them through Moses instead of by way of His audible voice. This was the inauguration of the dispensation of the Law, concerning which we read, "And it came to pass on the third day in the morning, that there were thunders and lightnings and a thick cloud upon the mountain, and the voice of the trumpet exceeding loud; so that all the people that was in the camp trembled. And Moses brought forth the people out of the camp to meet

with God; and they stood at the nether part of the mount.
And Mount Sinai was altogether on a smoke, because the
Lord descended upon it in fire: and the smoke thereof ascended as the smoke of a furnace, and the whole mount
quaked greatly" (Ex. 19:16-18).

The descriptive scene which we have just quoted from the
Bible was what the children of Israel experienced in the
wilderness at the giving of the Law. The thing that is of
interest is that various symbols of fear rather than of peace
were used to introduce the Law: thunder, lightning, thick
clouds, loud trumpet, smoke and the quaking of the mountain.
There is nothing in these verses that speaks of hope or peace,
nor that would cause the natural man to desire to approach
unto the Mount. It is such as would put fear and terror into
man. These were outward symbols of the Law.

Now, there neither was nor is anything wrong with the
Law, itself. It was given by God. It was His divine Law —
a Law that revealed His holiness and His holy requirements.
The trouble was not with the Law, but with man, — man in
his sinfulness. Man was undone before a holy God. There
was nothing in the Law that could make the one coming to
God perfect. In fact, the Law was not given to perfect man,
but rather that man might recognize how undone he really
is before a holy God. "The Law, as given at Sinai, brought
out the exceeding sinfulness of sin. Human sin had existed
before, but the utterance of Sinai brought it forth into
prominence before men, and stripping it of all disguise, made
it appear as it really is — sin exceeding sinful, the blackness
of darkness forever."[10]

Thus, the Law was given to show to man that he is undone
and unable, in himself, to stand before a holy God. The
natural heart causes man to think well of himself, but God
knew that "the heart of man is deceitful above all things,
and desperately wicked" (Jer. 17:9), therefore, He used these
vivid symbols at Sinai to show that all of man's "righteousnesses are as filthy rags" (Isa. 64:6).

---

[10] *Nicholson, op. cit.,* page 61.

The Psalmist, David, asked, "Who shall ascend unto the hill of the Lord? or who shall stand in his holy place?" He answered, "He that hath clean hands, and a pure heart; who hath not lifted up his soul unto vanity, nor sworn deceitfully" (Ps. 24:3, 4). But who of us can speak of a clean and a pure heart apart from Golgotha's provision? The Law was necessary in order to bring man to his knees and to help him realize his lost condition.

"What shall we say then? Is the law sin? God forbid. Nay, I had not known sin, but by the law: for I had not known lust, except the law had said, Thou shalt not covet" (Rom. 7:7). Let us, again, emphasize that there is nothing wrong with the Law. The trouble lies in man. Man, in his sin, is unable to live up to the holiness that God requires, and must accept the doom that was pronounced at Sinai by these symbols of dread and fear, or take refuge at Mount Golgotha, where God, through the sacrifice of His Son, speaks peace and forgiveness.

The terrors at Sinai were not the reality of the wrath of God upon the sinfulness of man, but only a scene that depicted God's attitude toward sin, and showed what it will be for the Christ-rejecter when the vengeance of God will be poured forth. These terrors were meant to instruct man to desire to be saved. This salvation is found in Him of whom the various legal sacrifices spoke in type.

GOLGOTHA'S EARTHQUAKE

There was another quaking. This time it was not to produce fear in the hearts of man, but to awaken faith and hope in Him, who, through His death on Mount Golgotha, was "blotting out the handwriting of ordinances [the Law] that was against us, which was contrary to us, and took it out of the way, nailing it to the cross, and having spoiled principalities and powers, he made a shew of them openly, triumphing over them in it" (Col. 2:14, 15). The earthquake at Golgotha was the response to the shout of victory from the lips of Jesus. Christ overcame the terror of the Law and all that the thunder, lightning, clouds, trumpets, smoke, and the quaking of the mountains signified. We now have a mountain of Grace whereunto all do well to approach. At Sinai no one, not even the animals, were allowed so much as to touch the mount, lest they be slain. But to the mount of Grace, and all that Golgotha signifies, all can come and find peace and forgiveness. The invitation of the gospel is, "The Spirit and the bride say, Come. And let him that heareth say, Come. And let him that is athirst come. And whosoever will, let him take of the water of life freely" (Rev. 22:17). It *was death to come near Sinai. It is death NOT to come* to Golgotha.

Here, at Golgotha, instead of hearing the trumpet of judgment, we hear the voice of the Son of God. What makes the difference? The death of Christ has atoned for man's sins. All that Sinai depicted with its wrath and fear had been placed upon the Sacrifice for the world. Because of this, all that will believe in Him, who became "the lamb of God that taketh away the sin of the world" (John 1:29), have peace with God.

"Sinai was the prophecy of Calvary — Calvary was a fulfilment of Sinai. . . . Sinai was God's inexorable voice of condemnation; Calvary, God's fatherly voice of pardon and peace."[11]

We see in this that mercy has triumphed by way of the cross over the vengeance of Sinai. The earthquake was God's seal of assurance that the redemptive work of Jesus Christ was completed.

THE SPIRITUAL SIGNIFICANCE OF THE EARTHQUAKE

Though "Palestine has from time to time immemorial been a country subject to earthquakes,"[12] this was no ordinary convulsion caused by natural forces. It was definitely miraculous in its method of working.

We see the miraculous in the *timing* of its occurrence. The

---

11 *Ibid.*, page 64.
12 Hastings, *op. cit.*, Vol. 1, page 634.

quake coincided with the shout of victory from the lips of Jesus. The darkness had just ended. The rending of the veil, a miraculous manifestation of the triumph of Christ's death over spiritual darkness, had either just taken place, or was at the very moment taking place (though independently of the earthquake). The rending of the veil signified the triumph of Christ over spiritual forces of darkness, and that access to God had been provided for man. But now the earth, that had been subject to the curse of sin since the fall of man, responded with the hope of its eventual deliverance from the curse through the death of the world's Redeemer. Thus, we could say that the quake was the earth's response to the Saviour's shout of triumph. That was no natural reaction of a convulsion within the earth's surface such as generally produced an earthquake, but it was a supernatural act of God.

Just one short week before this day of crucifixion, as Jesus had His royal entrance into Jerusalem the multitude was shouting, "Saying, Blessed be the King that cometh in the name of the Lord: peace in heaven, and glory in the highest. And some of the Pharisees from among the multitude said unto him, Master, rebuke thy disciples. And he answered and said unto them, I tell you that, if these should hold their peace, the *stones would immediately cry out*" (Luke 19:38-40). The entrance into Jerusalem that seemed to be a *triumphal entrance* turned out to be a *tragic entrance.* The death on the cross, that seemed to be a *tragic death,* turned out to be a *triumphant death,* for now the stones did cry out. The people now were silent, but the rocks cried out a testimony to the deity of the One who had been crucified. It was an indication of triumph.

It is believed, by some, that the earthquake shook the temple, and thus caused the rent in the veil. If that were the case, some other reference to damage done to the temple and to the city of Jerusalem would certainly be given to us in the Biblical account. It was indicated in the previous chapter that the rent in the veil was independent of the earthquake, though it is not impossible that it happened at the very same moment. It was the Lord's doing. The quaking of the earth, with its consequent rending of the rocks and opening of the graves, is full of instruction for all of us.

WHAT THE RENDING OF THE ROCKS INDICATED

When Adam and Eve had failed under the test in the garden of Eden, God said to Adam, "Because thou hast hearkened unto the voice of thy wife, and hast eaten of the tree, of which I commanded thee, saying, Thou shalt not eat of it: *cursed is the ground* for thy sake; in sorrow shalt thou eat of it all the days of thy life; thorns also and thistles shall it bring forth to thee" (Gen. 3:17, 18). From then on there has been a curse upon the earth. The thorns and weeds which we see and which cause us so much trouble are all due to the sin of man. The fear that is in animals and in all living creatures came because of man's failure to obey God. The earth with all of its creation shared in the curse of sin.

When Jehovah created Adam and Eve, He was to be King over the earth, living in that blissful fellowship with His creation, especially man, which He did enjoy for a time. This wonderful relationship was marred by sin. By man's disobedience sin entered into the world (Rom. 5:12) and brought a curse upon the entire earth. Wherever man has set his foot he has carried the curse of sin with him. But God is not through with this earth. He will yet rule as King of kings, and Lord of lords. Though, in the first coming of Christ as the Messiah and redeemer, He was rejected and crucified, through his death He paved the way to restore the earth to the condition which He had originally purposed. It was this anticipation that caused this convulsion of JOY to ring forth from the rocks — the earth's response to the redemptive work of Christ.

To this agreed Lange, when he said, "Rending of the rocks testified of His power and proved that earthly nature itself has experienced the influence of the suffering of death."[13]

"What does all this imply? Something great and glorious. The death of the Mediator has decided the future of the old world. It is, with all its concerns, devoted to destruction and awaits a great and comprehensive change. . . .The present creation is not what it was originally. The blood of the Lamb demands the restoration of the original state of created things. And the quaking of the earth to its very foundations, the tottering of the hills and mountains, the rending of the rocks which attended the Lord's death, all these are nothing else but an amen of Almighty God to the demand of the blood of His Son."[14]

Thus it was that the earth shared with man in the redemption that is in Christ Jesus. The Apostle Paul made this clear in his Epistle to the church in Rome when he said, "For the earnest expectation of the creature [creation] waiteth for the manifestation of the sons of God. For the creature [creation] was made subject to vanity, not willingly, but by reason of him who hath subjected the same in hope. Because the creature (creation) itself also shall be delivered from the bondage of corruption into the glorious liberty of the children of God. For we know that the whole creation groaneth and travaileth in pain together until now" (Rom. 8:19-22). Just as the earth was subjected to the curse of sin caused by the first Adam, so the same earth, with all of its creation, will share in the redemptive work of the Last Adam. Just as we must wait for the second coming of Christ to experience the full redemption that has been purchased for us, so the earth must wait for the coming of Christ when He will reign as Kings of kings, and Lord of lords. The earth's deliverance will be complete when Christ sets up His earthly millennial Kingdom.

That the earth's creatures will be affected by the millennial reign of Christ is seen in the many prophetic portions

---

13 *Op. cit.*, page 324.
14 Krummacher, *op. cit.*, page 413, 414.

that portray to us the general conditions on the earth during that time. I will quote just a few passages. "And there shall come forth a rod out of the stem of Jesse, and a Branch shall grow out of his roots: And the Spirit of the Lord shall rest upon him. . . . And righteousness shall be the girdle of his loins, and faithfulness the girdle of his reins. The wolf also shall dwell with the lamb, and the leopard shall lie down with the kid; and the calf and the young lion and the fatling together; and a little child shall lead them. And the cow and the bear shall feed; their young ones shall lie down together; and the lion shall eat straw like the ox. And the sucking child shall play on the hole of the asp, and the weaned child shall put his hand on the cockatrice' den. They shall not hurt nor destroy in all my holy mountain: for the earth shall be full of the knowledge of the Lord, as the waters cover the sea" (Isa. 11:1, 2, 5-9). "The wolf and the lamb shall feed together, and the lion shall eat straw like the bullock: and dust shall be the serpent's meat. They shall not hurt nor destroy in all my holy mountain, saith the Lord" (Isa. 65:25).

In the above quotations from the book of Isaiah we see that the nature of the animal world will be affected by the reign of Christ. This was secured for them through the atoning death of Christ. In the following quotations we see that the earth [soil] will also be transformed.

"The wilderness and the solitary place shall be glad for them: and the desert shall rejoice, and blossom as the rose. It shall blossom abundantly, and rejoice even with joy and singing: the glory of Lebanon shall be given unto it, the excellency of Carmel and Sharon, they shall see the glory of the Lord, and the excellency of our God . . . for in the wilderness shall waters break out, and streams in the desert. And the parched ground shall become a pool, and the thirsty land springs of water: in the habitation of dragons, where each lay, shall be grass with reeds and rushes" (Isa. 35:1, 2, 6, 7) ."For ye shall go out with joy, and be led forth with peace: the mountains and the hills shall break forth before you into singing, and all the trees of the field shall clap their hands. Instead of the thorn shall come up the fir tree, and instead of the brier shall come up the myrtle tree: and it shall be to the Lord for a name, for an everlasting sign that shall not be cut off" (Isa. 55:12, 13).

Let these quotations suffice to show to us that the day is coming when not only the redeemed of all ages and nations will enjoy the blessing of the Lord's provision, but also all of God's creation, likewise, will be at peace. All of this was included in that sacrifice of Christ on the cross. That is why the earth responded with the quake at the time of Christ's death.

THE MEANING OF THE OPEN GRAVES

Let us now take a look at the significance of the second part of this miracle — the opening of the graves. We call this the second part only because in it we find some new teaching that is not included in the general rending of the rocks due to the earthquake. This, also, has to do with the manifestation of Christ's Messiahship.

It does seem that the immediate purpose of the earthquake was the opening of the graves, for it was when the rocks rent that the graves were opened.

It must be remembered that the mode of burial was different among the Jews of that day from that which is commonly practiced today. "Graves or sepulchres were most commonly made, among the Jews, in solid rocks or in caves of rock. The rending of the rocks, therefore, would lay them open. The graves were *opened* by the earthquake...."[15]

As these places of burial were hewn out in these rocks, a body would be placed in the sepulchre, and a large flat rock would be placed against the opening to seal in the body. Thus it was, when the convulsion of the earth caused the rocks to rend, these stones or rocks, placed in front of the graves, would be wrenched away, exposing the bodies

---

15 Barnes, *op. cit.*, page 314.

buried in them. This is confirmed by Schaff in notes quoted in *Lange's Commentary on Matthew.*[16]

Whether graves in other places than in the general area of Jerusalem, also, were opened we are not told. But by conjecture, we may presume that it was only around Jerusalem that graves were actually opened, for it tells us that the saints that arose came into the Holy City (Matt. 27:53).

That there was a burial place near Golgotha is told to us by John in his Gospel account. "Now in the place where he was crucified there was a garden, and in the garden a new sepulchre, wherein was never man yet laid. There laid they Jesus therefore..." (John 19:41, 42). It is very probable that a number of others were buried in this same burial garden.

What graves were opened? How many were opened? That, the Bible does not tell us, but Bishop Nicholson contended that it was only the graves of the saints that were opened.[17] But that is not what Matthew expressly said. Note, again, the clear statement of Matthew. "And the earth did quake, and the rocks rent; and the graves were opened; and many bodies of the saints which slept arose, and came out of the graves after his resurrection" (Matt. 27:51-53). It does not even by conjecture suggest that only certain graves of certain saints were opened. However, *it is* clearly stated that *only* certain saints arose. It does not rob the significance of the miracle at all by not confining the opening of the graves to only certain saints. The basic teaching for us still remains. In fact, it seems to emphasize rather than lessen the force of the meaning.

There are differences of opinion among Bible students whether these saints came to life at the death of Christ and remained in the graves until after His resurrection, or if they came to life and came out of the graves simultaneously at the time of Christ's resurrection. I quote the following. The sleeping saints, "according to the usual punc-

---

16 Page 527.
17 *Op. cit.,* pages 59 and 72.

tuation in our version, were quickened into resurrection life at the moment of their Lord's death, but lay in their graves till His resurrection, when they came forth. But it is far more natural as we think, and consonant with other scriptures, to understand that only the graves were opened, probably by the earthquake, at our Lord's death, and this only in preparation for subsequent exit of those who slept in them, when the spirit of life should enter into them from their risen Lord, and along with Him they should come forth, trophies of His victory over the grave."[18]

It does not seem to me that the punctuation in any way requires us to say that they came to life at Christ's death and waited in the graves until His resurrection. Rather, their resurrection and coming forth from the graves are definitely linked with the resurrection of Jesus. There was no RESURRECTION of saints until after Christ was risen from the dead. He was the "firstfruits" of them that slept.

Continuing the above quotation, we read: "Thus, in the opening of the grave at the moment of the Redeemer's expiring, there was a glorious symbolical proclamation that the death which had just taken place had 'swallowed up death in victory,' and whereas the saints that slept in them were awakened only by their risen Lord, to accompany Him out of the tomb, it was fitting that the Prince of Life should be *first* that should rise from the dead."[19]

This, then, introduces us to the spiritual meaning of the opened graves. Just as the earthquake, with the rending rocks, was creation's response to the completed redemption, so the opening of the graves was death's response to its defeat in Christ's triumphant shout from the cross. "The miracle teaches how, by the work of Calvary, Christ has power and authority to reconquer from the grasp of death the life He once created."[20] It was the atonement of Christ that set the prisoners free. The *resurrection* was God's seal

---

[18] Jamieson, Fausset and Brown, *op. cit.*, page 129.
[19] *Ibid.*, page 129.
[20] *A Preacher's Homiletical Commentary on the Gospel of Matthew*, page 639.

of approval and acceptance of this atonement. Thus, the opened graves speak of His triumph over the grave. Through the atoning death the obstacle that had existed between us and immortality had been done away.

"His death had set wide open the prison doors, called off the guards, and left the way free. His resurrection was the use of that freedom.

"His death secured for His people their resurrection blessedness, in that it abolished the hindrances to life. His resurrection was the bestowal of that blessedness upon His people.

"His death is our judicial deliverance: His resurrection our actual deliverance.

"His death is our pardon; His resurrection the receipted certificate of that pardon.

"His death made Hades open; His resurrection, Hades empty. His death is the grave torn asunder; His resurrection is the dead bodies of His saints walking forth from their graves in the life incorruptible and eternal!"[21]

The opening of the graves was symbolic. But, it actually happened, and it was not a product of tradition of the days when Matthew wrote, as some would have us believe. This occurrence was symbolic of Christ's victory over the cause of death, over sin, and, thus, instructs us by use of the open grave that "as in Adam all die, even so in Christ shall all be made alive" (I Cor. 15:22). Thus, to confine the open graves to saints only would indicate that there will be a resurrection for saints only, and that all others will remain in the grave. This would be contrary to the words of Paul where he said, "In Christ shall all be made alive." The resurrection of the saints at Christ's resurrection indicates that the saints will arise first (I Thess. 4:13-17), and after that, at the appointed time, Christ will bring forth the ungodly from the graves. This agrees with the words of Jesus, Himself, when He taught about the resurrection: "Marvel not at this: for the hour is coming, in the which all that are in

---

21 Nicholson, *op. cit.*, pages 83, 84.

the graves shall hear his voice, and shall come forth: they that have done good, unto the resurrection of life: and they that have done evil, unto the resurrection of damnation" (John 5:28, 29). It is through the death of Christ that *all* will be raised from the dead, each one according to their relationship with the Lord.

The opening of the graves is a prophecy or an assurance that there *will be* a resurrection. All this is given to us symbolically. We must await the *resurrection day* for the full and complete fulfillment of this prophecy. Just as we, as believers, are already set free from death, as we are risen with Christ through saving faith in Him, but must await the resurrection morn of the saints to experience the reality of it, so also the open graves did not permit all saints to come forth, but just chosen ones, to give us assurance that "faithful is he that calleth you, who also will do it" (I Thess. 5:24).

Again, I would like to emphasize that "through death he might destroy him that had the power of death, that is, the devil" (Heb. 2:14). So, at the moment of His death, this victory was declared and His Messiahship was confirmed by the rocks rending apart and leaving many graves open.

Hallelujah, What a Saviour!

> "Wonderful death, for it meant not defeat,
> Calvary made His great mission complete,
> Wrought our redemption, and when He arose,
> Banished forever the last of our foes.
>
> "Wonderful hope, He is coming again,
> Coming as King o'er the nations to reign;
> Glorious promise, His Word cannot fail,
> His righteous kingdom at last must prevail!"
>   — A. H. Ackley

4. The Blood and the Water

"But one of the soldiers with a spear pierced His side, and forthwith came there out blood and water" (John 19:34).

The darkness of three hours had passed. This was followed by the rending of the veil from the top to the bottom, and by the earthquake that rent the rocks and opened the graves. The spirit of Jesus had departed. This series of miraculous events brought forth the testimony from one of the Roman soldiers, "Truly this was the Son of God" (Matt. 27:54).

It was unusual for one who was crucified to die so soon. Frequently that one would live on in the stupor of the anguish and pain for a full day or two or even for as long as three days. Even Pilate was surprised to learn that Jesus was already dead, for we read, "And now when even was come, because it was the preparation, that is, the day before the sabbath, Joseph of Arimathaea, an honourable counsellor, which also waited for the kingdom of God, came, and went in boldly unto Pilate, and craved the body of Jesus. And Pilate marvelled if he were already dead" (Mark 15:42-44).

BREAKING THE LEGS OF THE CRUCIFIED

Just prior to this, "The Jews therefore, because it was the preparation, that the bodies should not remain upon the cross on the sabbath day, (for that sabbath day was an high day), besought Pilate that their legs might be broken, and that they might be taken away. Then came the soldiers, and brake the legs of the first, and of the other which was crucified with him. But when they came to Jesus, and saw that he was dead already, they brake not his legs: but one of the soldiers with a spear pierced his side, and forthwith came there out blood and water" (John 19:31-34).

The Jews were more concerned about the outward observance of the Sabbath than they were about the Righteous Son of God whom they had caused to be crucified. Herein, also, it was true that they were omitting "the weightier matters of the law, judgment, mercy, and faith . . ." (Matt. 23:23). In order to hasten death, so that the body of Jesus and of the two crucified with Him would not linger on the cross during their "high day," they asked to have the legs broken of those who were crucified.

Some writers say that this practice of breaking the legs did not hasten death, but just increased the suffering. But by increasing their suffering they felt justified in hastening death by later thrusting a spear into their sides which would bring death by bleeding. The breaking of the legs, with its awful pain, was to make up for the shorter duration of suffering on the cross.

When the soldiers, at the request of the Jews and the permission of Pilate, came to the two who were crucified with Christ, "they brake the legs." The breaking of the legs usually was by crushing the legs with a club or hammer. With the awful pain of being crucified and the fever which increased as the moments went by, the breaking of the legs was a definite climax of the tortuous death.

THE LEGS OF JESUS NOT BROKEN

"But when they came to Jesus, and saw that he was dead already, they brake not His legs." Jesus was the central figure on Golgotha's hill that day, central as though He were the greatest sinner. In a certain sense this might be said to be true, as He there bore the sins of the whole world, even the sins of the malefactors who were crucified with Him. This central figure had complete control over His own life. When He had fulfilled *all;* when He had drained the cup given by the Father to the very last dreg, there remained nothing for which He needed to continue His suffering, and thus, He gave up His life and committed His spirit unto the Father. Here the reality of Christ's statement is seen, ". . . I lay down my life, . . . No man taketh it from me, but I lay it down of myself" (John 10:17, 18).

Consequently, when they found that He was dead already, they did not break His legs. This was in definite fulfilment of the prophecies concerning Him. The prophet said, "He keepth all His bones: not one of them is broken" (Psalm 34:20). This was further indicated, in type, in the Passover lamb. It was commanded, "neither shall ye break a bone thereof" (Ex. 12:46b). In giving the command for the annual observance of the Passover, God commanded, "They shall leave none of it unto the morning, nor break any bone of it: according to all the ordinances of the passover they shall keep it" (Num. 9:12). So, in order for Christ to be the fulfilment of the Passover lamb, it was necessary that not a bone be broken.

THEY PIERCED HIS SIDE

When they found Him dead, "one of the soldiers with a spear pierced his side." This was ordinarily done later to hasten the death of those whose legs had been broken. The breaking of bones, as mentioned before, was not intended to bring death, but "the breaking of the bones was followed by a *coup de grace,* by sword, lance, or stroke, which immediately put an end to what remained of life."[1] Since the life had already departed from Jesus, there was no point in breaking the legs, but seemingly, to make certain of death, the soldiers pierced His side. Though the word "pierced" as given by John simply means "pricked," it is evident from John 20:27, "reach hither thy hand, and thrust it into my side," that it was a deep gash, such as was made by the jagged edge of a Roman spear.

This, also, was in fulfilment of prophecy. One of the Old Testament prophets declared, "And they shall look upon me whom they have pierced" (Zach. 12:10). From the words of

---

[1] Edersheim, *op. cit.,* p. 613.

John (19:35-37), it would seem that the main reason for recording the event of not breaking His bones and of the piercing of His side was to show that even in this that the prophecy was fulfilled; thus showing that He truly was the Messiah and Redeemer He had declared Himself to be.

In connection with the piercing of His side, a strange phenomenon took place, which, I believe, John gave as another "sign" of the supernatural quality of the Person and the death that he and many others had witnessed. However, John did not go ahead to explain this "sign," although it is evident that he regarded it to be of great significance. He stated, "But one soldier with a spear pierced his side, and forthwith came there out *blood and water*" (John 19:34).

It is my sincere belief that the only explanation for the blood and water is to declare it to be a miracle, even as the other events already discussed, in connection with the crucifixion.

EXPLANATION OF THE BLOOD AND WATER

Various naturalistic explanations of the death of Christ and the cause of the flow of blood and water are given by eminent doctors and theologians, where the opinion of one is as varied as that of the other. The writing that has possibly received the most prominence throughout the past century is *A Treatise on the Physical Cause of the Death of Christ,* by Dr. William Stroud, written in 1847.

Stroud explained the death of Christ by suggesting that while He hung on the cross His heart ruptured. The ruptured heart, in turn, caused a large effusion of blood into the pericardium. There the blood separated into the more solid form and liquid parts. When the pericardium was pierced by the soldiers, it was the more solid form and the liquid that flowed forth from the side of Christ.

B. F. Westcott objected to this interpretation because, as he points out, "such separation is evidence of beginning of corruption, and Christ did not see corruption."[2]

_____
[2] *The Gospel According to St. John,* page 279.

Hoffmann said that "the bleeding away of the dead One had been so complete, that at last not blood, but water flowed, and this was, to the apostle, a proof that Jesus' corpse remained exempt from corruption, which begins with the decomposition of the blood."[3]

Lange pointed out the difficulty of Stroud's naturalistic interpretation when he said that blood does not flow out of a dead body freely, "neither does it separate into blood and water (plasma and serum) as it does in a vessel after venesection."[4]

It seems to me that we search in vain for any natural explanation for His death. May I refer you again to the words of Christ, Himself. "I lay down my life . . . I lay it down of myself." The cause of His death was the miraculous dismissal of His spirit. The miracle was that, at the moment he had completed all that was spoken concerning Him, He committed His spirit to the Father. The moment He died, the spirit was absent from the body.

So, also, the "blood and water" that flowed from His side cannot be explained by the natural mind. It was a miracle. As were the other miracles which were connected with His death, so *this* miracle is full of instruction for us.

VIEWS OF EARLY CHURCH FATHERS

It is of interest to inject here some of the thoughts of the early church fathers on the significance of the Scripture portion at hand.

Westcott pointed out that recently discovered works of Marcarius Manges, a notable Greek, has an interesting note on this passage, though the text is, as he indicated, possibly corrupt: "One of the soldiers pierced the side . . . in order that when blood flowed and water in a gushing stream, by the blood they may be delivered who occupied the place of

---

[3] In his *Schriftbew.* II. 1, page 490, quoted from footnote in *Critical and Exegetical Commentary on the New Testament,* the Gospel of John, Vol. II, by Heinrich A. W. Meyer, page 357.

[4] *Lange's Commentary on John, Critical, Doctrinal, and Homiletical.*

captivity, and by water they may be washed who bear the stripes of sin. Certainly this hath been done not without purpose, but of Providence, as though the divine forethought laid down that it should come to pass: for since (from the side came the origin of sin) it was necessary that from the side should flow the source of salvation: from the side came the sting, from the side the spring: from the side the malady, from the side the cure."

Ambrose, in De Sacram. 5:1 says, "Why water? Why blood? Water to cleanse: blood to redeem. Why from the side? Because, whence came the guilt, thence came the grace. The guilt was through the woman: the grace was through the Lord Jesus Christ."

Rupert of Dentz writes in Comm. in John XIII pp. 365f, "We are redeemed by blood: we are washed by water. . . . The Lord was baptized in His own passion, and when already dead by that issue enabled us to share in His saving death. . . . Therefore not blood only, nor water only, flowed from the Saviour's side; because the divine order of our salvation requires both. For we were not redeemed from this that He should possess us such as we were before. . . . In order then that there might be that by which we could be washed from our sins, water, which could only wash bodily impurities, was united to blood, which is the price of our redemption, and from that union obtained virtue and power to be worthy of cooperation with the Holy Spirit and to wash away the invisible impurities of sin." Here, again, we see the combined work of His death — the redemption through His blood and the cleansing by water.

Augustine connected the death of Christ, the last Adam, with the first Adam regarding the creation of Eve. "The sleep of the man (Adam) was the death of Christ: for He hung lifeless on the Cross, His side was pierced by the spear, and thence flowed forth blood and water, which we know to be the sacraments by which the church (the antitype of Eve) is built up (de Civ. XXII. c.17) ."

Augustine is not the only one who interprets the blood and water to mean the two ordinances of the church—Bap-

tism and the Lord's Supper. For Chrysostom, a Greek, in
Hom. LXXXV. *in loc,* says, "Not without purpose or by
chance did those springs come forth, but because the church
consisteth of these two together. And those initiated know it,
being regenerated by water and nourished by the Blood
and Flesh. Hence, the Sacraments take their beginning; in
order that when thou drawest near to the awful cup thou
mayest so approach, as drinking from the very side."

Though there undoubtedly is a great degree of truth in
the interpretations which these early Church Fathers have
placed on this miracle at Golgotha, it seems that they missed
its basic interpretation—that Christ's death was the fulfilment
of all that the Law required, because He was the only Perfect
Sacrifice. Instead of the blood and the water referring to
the ordinances of the church, the ordinances of the church
point back to the symbolic value of what the blood and the
water teach us.

Origen, in his commentary on Galatians (V. 268 ed. Lom-
matzsch) simply treated this sign as a proof of the reality of
the Lord's body. To this agreed Westcott, in dealing with
the miraculous phenomenon. "The issuing of the blood and
water from His side, must therefore be regarded as a sign
of life in death. It showed both His true humanity and (in
some mysterious sense) the permanence of His human life.
Though dead, dead in regard to our mortal life, the Lord
yet lived; and as He hung upon the cross He was shown
openly to be the source of double cleansing and vivifying
power, which followed from His death and life."[5]

Theophylact believed that "the blood is a mark that the
Crucified was man, but the water that He was more than
man, that He was God."[6]

It would appear from the words of John (19:35-37), that
this was recorded as an evidence not only of His death but
also as an evidence of His Messiahship and Deity, for the
blood and the water are symbols of His actual mission on

---

[5] The quotations are from B. F. Westcott, *The Gospel According to St.
John,* page 279ff.
[6] *Op cit.,* page 279.

earth. He came to bring "redemption through his blood, the forgiveness of sin" (Eph. 1:7), and "that he might sanctify and cleanse it [the church] with the washing of the water by the word" (Eph. 5:26). Thus, we are "not redeemed with corruptible things as silver and gold, ... but with the precious blood of Christ, as of a lamb without blemish and without spot" (I Peter 1:18, 19). Why? "That you should shew forth the praises of him, who hath called you out of darkness into his marvelous light" (I Peter 2:9), and further, "that he might present it to himself a glorious church, not having spot, or wrinkle, or any such thing; but that it should be holy and without blemish" (Eph. 5:27).

USE OF BLOOD AND WATER IN CEREMONIAL WORSHIP

The significance of *blood* and *water* is seen in its use in ceremonial worship under the Law. It is there that we must turn in order to find its basic meaning. The blood and water is another outward sign that Christ's death was the complete fulfilment of all that the Law demanded, even as the rending of the veil declared the end of the dispensation of ceremonial worship. The ceremonies of the Law were used as a picture of the cleansing which Christ would provide through His death. This was a fulfilment of the words of the prophet, "In that day there shall be a fountain opened to the house of David and to the inhabitants of Jerusalem for sin and for uncleanness" (Zech. 13:1). "Therefore with joy shall ye draw water out of the wells of salvation" (Isa. 12:3).

In the worship at the Tabernacle, as man approached God, there was, first the brazen altar of sacrifice where blood was shed for the expiation of the sins of the people. Next, in the approach to the presence of God, was the water laver just at the entrance to the Tabernacle. This was a place for cleansing after the sacrifice had been brought and before the entering into the Tabernacle to perform the priestly service.

All of this is significant in the light of the phenomenon of the "blood and water" that flowed forth from the side of

Christ. His death completely fulfilled every detail of what the Law spoke or demanded. Hence, the blood would speak to us of the remission of our sins, for we read, "without shedding of blood is no remission" (Heb. 9:22). The water teaches us that, not only are our sins forgiven through His death, but also, it is His death that makes it possible for us to have our lives cleansed daily, to ever be clean for fellowship and worship. This is the truth conveyed by John in his First Epistle. Remember, this epistle was written to believers. He said, "If we walk in the light, as he is in the light, we have fellowship one with another, and the blood of Jesus Christ his Son cleanseth us from all sin" (I John 1:7). This is a continuous cleansing we experience moment by moment as we walk in the light. This is the truth taught by the water. Also, "If we confess our sins, he is faithful and just to forgive us our sins, and to cleanse us from all unrighteousness" (I John 1:9).

Thus, I would say that the blood and the water teach us that the death of Christ fulfilled all that the brazen altar, with its blood sacrifices, and the water laver, with its cleansing, signified. Through His death we are made fit subjects to enter into the presence of God, not only to fellowship in prayer in the holy place, before the veil, but to enter into the Holiest of all, into the very presence of God.

JOHN'S USE OF THE WORDS, "BLOOD AND WATER"

The meaning of this sign-miracle becomes more understandable as we see how the words "blood" and "water" are used by John elsewhere in his writings. Let us consider, first of all, the word *blood*.

Blood is given by John as a symbol of natural life. He said, "Which were born, not of blood [in contrast to the spiritual birth of the previous verse], ... but of God" (John 1:13). He is simply saying that through our natural blood we inherit the natural life, which does not make us members of the spiritual family of God.

After Christ's great discourse on being the Bread of Life,

He turned to the great multitude which had followed Him because they had eaten of the bread He had multiplied, and said, "Verily, verily, I say unto you, Except ye eat the flesh of the Son of man, and drink his blood, ye have no life in you. Whoso eateth my flesh, and drinketh my blood, hath eternal life; and I will raise him up at the last day. For my flesh is meat indeed and my blood is drink indeed. He that eateth my flesh and drinketh my blood, dwelleth in me, and I in him" (John 6:53-56). Since "the life of the flesh is in the blood" (Lev. 17:11), He was showing that His body, prepared by God and having natural life, was prepared for sacrifice. Through this death it was possible for Him to communicate the virtue of His life to those who believe in Him. That it was necessary for Christ to die in order to pass on to us the virtue of His life is seen where Jesus said, "Except a corn of wheat fall into the ground and die, it abideth alone: but if it die, it bringeth forth much fruit" (John 12:24). His blood, then, stands for life, and this life must be poured out to provide life for us. "Unto him that loved us, and washed us from our sins in his own blood" (Rev. 1:5b).

In Revelation 5:9, John takes us to a scene in heaven where we read, "and they sung a new song, saying, Thou art worthy to take the book, and to open the seals thereof: for thou wast slain, and hast redeemed us to God by thy blood out of every kindred, and tongue, and people, and nation." Another scene is found in Revelation 7:14, "And he said unto me, These are they which came out of great tribulation, and have washed their robes, and made them white in the blood of the Lamb."

These verses indicate to us that great stress is laid upon the importance of the *blood*. The doctrine of blood atonement has always been against or contrary to human nature. This manifested itself in the first human family on earth. Cain preferred to bring an offering of the fruit of the land rather than of the firstling of the flock. People who do not want to have anything to do with the blood of Christ in this life will not have anything to do with the Life He offers throughout eternity. Christ, and the blood that was shed, will be the theme of conversation and praise in heaven.

Blood, then, as John used it, speaks of His life poured forth to provide a full and complete redemption from our sins, even as typified in the ceremonial sacrifices under the Law.

The *water*, in contrast, is the symbol of spiritual life. "But whosoever drinketh of the *water* that I shall give him shall never thirst; but the water that I shall give him shall be in him a well of water springing up into everlasting life" (John 4:14). This is further shown when Christ said, "He that believeth on me, as the scripture hath said, out of his belly [innermost being] shall flow rivers of living water. (But this spake he of the Spirit, which they that believe on him should receive)" (John 7:38, 39). Christ, here, is definitely linking the water with the spiritual life that becomes ours at the moment we are born again. Christ declared His Spirit to be *living water,* and Christ by His death provided for the out-pouring of the Spirit that gives life. This *life*-giving water satisfies. Jesus said, "Whosoever drinketh of the water that I shall give him shall never thirst; but the *water* that I shall give him shall be in him a well of water springing up into everlasting life" (John 4:14). This agrees with the words of our risen Saviour when He gave this wonderful promise, "I will give unto him that is athirst of the water of life freely" (Rev. 21:6), and "Let him that is athirst come. And whosoever will, let him take of the water of life freely" (Rev. 22:17).

Water, thus, has a two-fold significance: the satisfying spiritual life which is offered to us through the death of Christ, and the cleansing from sin which He now gives to all who come to Him. Though the cleansing is consequent on the blood that was shed, the symbol still remains. Water speaks of life and cleansing.

Therefore, by the sign of "blood and water," we are brought to realize that "it is through the death of Christ, and His new life by death, that the life of the Spirit and the support of the whole complex fulness of human life is assured to man. The symbols of the Old Covenant found their fulfilment in the New."[7]

John, again, referred to the "blood and water" in his First Epistle: "This is he that came by water and blood, even Jesus Christ; not by water only, but by water and blood" (I John 5:6). It is evident that John is here referring to the incident at Golgotha where blood and water came forth from His side.

It was absolutely necessary for Christ to come in likeness of man in order to provide a *blood* sacrifice for the lost human race. His was a real body, composed of flesh, bones and blood. It was a special body in that it was prepared by the Father. Quoting Psalm 40:6-7, the writer of Hebrews gave this testimony of our Lord, "Sacrifice and offering thou wouldst not, but *a body hast thou prepared me*" (Heb. 10:5). It was in order to provide an atonement for the sins of mankind that Christ came in this especially prepared human body.

THE DOCTRINE OF BLOOD ATONEMENT

There is a great neglect today in the proclamation and teaching about the blood and the water. The doctrine of blood atonement is an unpopular teaching to the natural man, because it is contrary to the pride of man. The acceptance of this doctrine immediately gives admission to the total depravity of man — that man is *totally* lost and unable to do anything of himself to obtain his salvation. This strips man of any righteousness of his own and reveals that his only help is in the grace of God. That is why, throughout generations, the teaching and the preaching of the blood have never been popular with those who seek to establish a righteousness of their own.

Salvation apart from *blood sacrifice* is foreign to the only revelation of God given to us. This is seen from the very beginning of the history of mankind. The Bible shows us that blood had to be shed to provide a covering for the naked bodies of our first parents after they had fallen into sin (Gen.

---

[7] *Ibid.*, page 279.

3:21). Ever since then, the only access to God has been by the way of the blood of an *innocent victim,* speaking always, in type, of the innocent, spotless Lamb of God, who was to be offered outside the camp, as a sacrifice, once and for all, for the sins of the world. The sacrifices that were brought by the Patriarchs before Sinai, and after the giving of the Law, all spoke of the blood that was to be poured forth on the Passover Day when our Redeemer, Himself, was to be the sacrifice.

"Blood!" you say, "What a repulsive thought!" To those who believe in the blood atonement it is the most *wonderful* word in all the world. It is a word that symbolizes deliverance from sin and its bondage — a word that spells hope for the damned — a word that means assurance for the fainthearted.

To *reject* the blood of Christ is to reject the *only* remedy for the malady of sin. To *neglect* the blood is equally disastrous. Those who neglect to proclaim the blood of Christ are as guilty before God as those who refuse to proclaim it. The only hope for man, lost in sin, is the blood that was shed as the atonement for his sin.

But let us notice here, John said that there was not only blood that came forth from His side, but water also. God was not satisfied that there should only be forgiveness of sins, but that there should be constant cleansing from every stain of sin, as well. The redemption that is in Christ Jesus is complete.

> "There is a fountain filled with blood
>   Drawn from Immanuel's veins;
> And sinners, plunged beneath that flood,
>   Lose all their guilty stains.
>
> "Dear dying Lamb, Thy precious blood
>   Shall never lose its power,
> Till all the ransomed Church of God
>   Be saved, to sin no more."
>   — Wm. Cowper

5. The Resurrection of Jesus Christ from the Dead

We have here another miracle! If miracles warrant comparison, we might well say that the resurrection of the Lord Jesus Christ was the greatest of all miracles. Yet, as James Orr so ably stated, "If Christ was what His Church has hitherto believed Him to be — the divine Son and Saviour of the world — there is no antecedent presumption against His resurrection; rather it is incredible that He should have remained the prey of death."[1] Thus, we could say that His resurrection was the natural outcome of being the Son of God, as was declared by Peter, "It was not possible that he should be holden of it [death]" (Acts 2:24).

It is interesting to note, as we read the Gospel account, that no one observed the actual resurrection. It is simply stated by the four Gospel narrators that He arose and that the grave was empty. The fact that He was not seen coming forth from the grave has often been used by critics as an attack on the truth of the resurrection. I believe that William Bancroft Hill is right in his analysis. He wrote: "If the story were fiction, we might expect it to begin with an account of Christ's coming forth from the tomb. Imagination would dwell on this, and picture it as seen by someone. Indeed, the late Apocryphal Gospel of Peter does describe how the guards and the Jewish elders, who are said to have been with them, saw 'three men coming forth from the tomb, two of them supporting the other, and a cross following them; and the heads of the two reached to heaven, but the head of the third overpassed the heavens. And they heard a voice from the

---

[1] *The Resurrection of Jesus,* page 14.

heavens, saying, "Didst thou preach to them that slept?" And a response *was heard* from the Cross, "Yea." ' "[2] It must be remembered that Matthew, who gave us the account of the guards, did not say that anyone of the guards saw Jesus, but that the moment the earth quaked and the angel appeared, "for fear of him the keepers did shake, and became as dead men" (Matt. 28:4). When the stone was rolled away, the tomb was empty.

All four Gospel writers agree that Jesus rose the third day, the first day of the week. Paul's testimony is in agreement with the four Evangelists in this, as seen in I Corinthians 15:3, "And rose again the third day, according to the scriptures."

THE GOSPEL ACCOUNTS OF THE RESURRECTION

At this point we want to pause long enough to compare the Gospel accounts of this event. Not every detail will be pointed out, but rather an attempt will be made to show the unity of the account.

All four accounts agree that Mary Magdalene was the leading personality in that early morning visit to the tomb. It is further agreed that it was after the Sabbath or on the first day of the week that they came to the tomb. Mark and Luke record for us the purpose of the visit — that of bringing spices which they had prepared to anoint Him.

Matthew, alone, gave the account of the earthquake and the descent of the angel from heaven to roll away the stone. Mark, Luke and John mentioned that Mary Magdalene and other women with her found the stone rolled away. Mark and Luke told of finding an empty tomb. John seems to indicate that all that Mary Magdalene saw was the stone rolled away.

Matthew, although he did not state that Mary Magdalene saw the empty tomb, recorded the message of the angel, "He is not here: for he is risen, as he said" (Matt. 28:6). Mark recorded the angelic message thus, "He is risen; he is not

---

[2] *The Resurrection of Jesus Christ,* page 40.

here: behold the place where they laid him" (Mark 16:6). John said that Mary saw the stone rolled away, and that he and Peter went into the tomb, and were convinced of His resurrection because of the arrangement of the grave clothes (we will discuss this in a separate chapter as one of the great miracles of Golgotha).

This is sufficient to show the agreement among the accounts we have that Christ truly had risen. We have the message of the angels and the empty tomb that point to the reality of this great truth.

It will also be noticed that Mary Magdalene seemingly had the foremost part in the account. Exactly who Mary Magdalene was cannot be stated with certainty. It is generally believed that she was the sinful woman of Luke 7:37, 38, who had much forgiven (vv. 47, 48). In the next chapter (8:1-3) we find that seven devils had been cast out of Mary Magdalene, and that she followed Christ and ministered to Him. She was probably from Magdala, on the Lake of Galilee, which town had a bad reputation. We find her at the cross, and other women with her. Here, at the grave on the first day of the week, she seemed to play the leading part. She certainly revealed in her acts the truth of what Jesus said concerning her, "Her sins, which are many, are forgiven; for she loved much" (v. 47a). She loved Him so much because so much had been forgiven.

The major testimony of the women at the tomb was that Christ actually arose. The differences in the accounts about the women at the tomb (which we will not discuss in this connection), indicates that they are incomplete, but by no means *contradictory*.[3] It should be noticed that there is a consistency in the report — the stone was rolled away and the tomb was empty. "There is not a hint anywhere that the fact of the empty tomb was ever questioned by either friend or foe. It would have been easy to question or disprove it when the apostles were boldly proclaiming the resurrection in Jerusalem a few weeks later. But no one appears to have

---

3 Orr, *op. cit.*, page 121.

done so."[4] The only weapon the enemy could use was the trumped up story that the body of Jesus had been stolen by the disciples (Matt. 28:11-15).

Though the accounts vary in detail, "the central fact — the empty grave, the message to the women, the appearances to the disciples, sustained as these were by the independent witness of Paul in I Corinthians 15:7, the belief of the whole Apostolic Church — stood secure."[5]

From all indications, no matter how the account is viewed, the event of the resurrection actually happened, even though critics have, because they cannot explain it, declared the account of the resurrection of Christ an addition; incorporating myths of death and resurrection of those in pagan religions.[6]

IMPORTANCE OF THE RESURRECTION

The importance of the resurrection of Jesus Christ from the dead cannot be overemphasized. Upon this rests our hope of acceptance before God. Our *faith* must also rest in His resurrection in order to be saved. "If thou shalt confess with thy mouth the Lord Jesus, and *believe* in thine heart that *God hath raised him from the dead,* thou shalt be saved" (Rom. 10:9).

"Christianity is the only religion that bases its claims of acceptance *upon* the resurrection of its Founder."[7] In this, our faith is unique. This takes our faith out of the realm of just another ethical code or religion, and places it in a position by itself — having a finality and an authority about its claims. "If Christ be not risen, then is your preaching vain, and your faith is also vain. . . . If Christ be not raised, your faith is vain; ye are yet in your sins" (I Cor. 15:14, 17). If the resurrection is removed from the gospel, the impact of its message is gone.

The importance of the resurrection is seen in the study of

---

4 *Ibid.,* page 127.
5 *Ibid.,* pages 11, 12.
6 See Origen, *Against Celsus* II. 55-58.
7 William Evans, *The Great Doctrines of the Bible,* page 84.

the book of Acts, where we see the prominence it held in
the ministry and the faith of the early church. It was the
very foundation of the hope of the church. This is evidenced
by just a few references to it from the book of Acts: Peter,
on the day of Pentecost, declared, "Him [Jesus], being delivered by the determinate counsel and foreknowledge of
God, ye have taken, and by wicked hands have crucified and
slain: *Whom God hath raised up,* having loosed the pains of
death: because it was not possible that he should be holden
of it....This Jesus hath God raised up, whereof we all are
witnesses" (Acts 2:23, 24, 32). In another sermon by Peter,
he said, "But ye denied the Holy One and the Just, and desired a murderer to be granted unto you; and killed the
Prince of life, *whom God hath raised from the dead;* whereof we are witnesses" (Acts 3:14, 15). In the fulness of the
Holy Spirit, as Peter addressed the Sanhedrin in Jerusalem,
he proclaimed with all authority, "Be it known unto you all,
and to all the people of Israel, that by the name of Jesus
Christ of Nazareth, whom ye crucified, *whom* God *raised
from the dead,* even by him doth this man stand here before
you whole" (Acts 4:10). In his message to the Gentiles in
the house of Cornelius, Peter said, "And we are witnesses of
all things which he [Jesus] did both in the land of the
Jews, and in Jerusalem; whom they slew and hanged on a
tree: *him God raised up* the third day, and shewed him
openly" (Acts 10:39, 40).

The Apostle Paul's message at Antioch in Pisidia was cen-
tered around this same theme, for he proclaimed, "And
though they found no cause of death in him, yet desired they
Pilate that he should be slain. And when they had fulfilled
all that was written of him, they took him down from the
tree, and laid him in a sepulchre. But *God raised him from
the dead*: and he was seen.... And as concerning that he
raised him up from the dead, now no more to return to corruption ..." (Acts 13:28-31, 34). These quotations are sufficient to show what place the faith in Christ's resurrection
had in the preaching and work of the early Church. "More

than one hundred times it is spoken of in the New Testament alone."[8]

The resurrection of Jesus Christ from the dead is the foundation and hope of the church and the assurance that we, too, are to be raised from the dead. It was this hope that made the early Christians willing to suffer for their faith. "A dead Christ might have been a teacher and wonder-worker, and remembered and loved as such. But only a Risen and Living Christ could be the Saviour, the Life and Life-giver — and as such preach to all men. . . . This is the foundation of the church, the inscription on the banner of her armies, the strength and comfort of every Christian heart, and the grand hope of humanity: The Lord is risen indeed."[9]

IT WAS A MIRACLE

The only explanation for the resurrection is to declare it to be a miracle. "The belief in the resurrection of Jesus was belief in a true miracle."[10] It is the miraculous that stands in the way of faith for the natural man. A miracle calls for God. This is possibly what Paul had in mind when he wrote, "Eye hath not seen, nor ear heard, neither have entered into the heart of [the natural] man, the things which God hath prepared for them that love him" (I Cor. 2:9). However, he goes on to make this explanation, "But God hath revealed them unto us by his Spirit" (v. 10). The natural man cannot understand a miracle. Paul continued a little later in the same chapter, "The natural man receiveth not the things of the Spirit of God" (v. 14). So it is with the resurrection. The natural mind cannot explain that which goes beyond his experience. To those of us, though not understanding, yet believing, the Holy Spirit has revealed the truth and the reality of it. The means used by the Holy Spirit to reveal these truths is through the Word of God. "The evidence [of Christ's resurrection] was not designed to satisfy scientific

---

8 Evans, *op. cit.*, page 85.
9 Edersheim, *op. cit.*, page 629.
10 Orr., *op. cit.*, page 35.

experts, but to produce faith in those 'chosen before of God' (Acts 10:40, 41), that they might be 'witnesses' to others."[11]

THE APPEARANCE OF CHRIST AFTER THE RESUR-RECTION

There are a number of appearances of Christ given in the Gospel records. From the outward appearance, it would seem at times that there are some discrepancies. This is caused partly by the individual records not being complete in themselves. Two writers may describe the same event, but from a different viewpoint. These are actually not discrepancies, but just an indication that *no one* author gives us a complete picture. They simply presented that which is essential to the message they have to proclaim.

In this connection I want to quote a footnote that Evans gives, where he is quoting Orr. "An instructive example is furnished in a recent issue of the *Bibliotheca Sacra*. A class in history was studying the French Revolution, and the pupils were asked to look the matter up, and report next day by what vote Louis XVI was condemned. Nearly half of the class reported that the vote was unanimous. A considerable number protested that he was condemned by a majority of one. A few gave the majority as 145 in a vote of 721. How utterly irreconcilable these reports seemed! Yet for each, the authority of reputable historians could be given. In fact, all were true, and the full truth was a combination of all three. On the first vote as to the king's guilt there was no contrary voice. Some tell only of this. The vote on the penalty was given individually, with reasons, and a majority of 145 declared for the death penalty, at once or after peace was made with Austria, or after confirmation by the people. The votes for immediate death were only 361 as against 360."[12]

The above example shows, to some degree, why there *seemingly* are discrepancies in the account of Christ's appear-

___

[11] *Ibid.*, page 147.
[12] *Op. cit.*, page 93, 94; quotation taken from Orr, *The Resurrection of Jesus.*

ances after His resurrection. No one writer gives us all the appearances. Some overlap in their report, and even in the places where they do report the same incident, they do not give all the details. Therefore, it is necessary to take into account all the reports and from that see the order of events.

There are differences of opinions among Bible teachers regarding the exact order of Christ's appearances to various people mentioned in the records of the Scriptures. I submit the following order, with full realization that there is room to differ on the exact order of His appearances:

1. To Mary, as she lingered at the grave, where she also was commanded to go tell the disciples (John 20:14-18)
2. To the other women on the way (Matt. 28:8-10)
3. To Simon Peter (Luke 24:34)
4. To the two on the way to Emmaus (Luke 24:13-31)
5. To the ten disciples (Luke 24:31-43; John 20:19-24)
6. To the Eleven (John 20:24-29)
7. To the seven disciples at Tiberias (John 21:1-23)
8. To more than 500 brethren (I Cor. 15:6)
9. To James (I Cor. 15:7)
10. To the disciples on the mount (Matt. 28:16-18; Acts 1:1-9)
11. To Paul (I Cor. 15:8)
12. To John (Rev. 1:10-19)

FALSE VIEWS OF THE RESURRECTION

The teaching that Jesus Christ arose from the dead has been a controversial subject in all ages since His life here on the earth. The critics have tried every possible attack to disprove and discredit the reality of this wonderful truth. There are two theories whereby the enemies of the gospel tried to disprove the reality of the resurrection that today are not as prevalent as they were a few decades ago. We do well, however, to take time to look at these attacks. The two referred to are: first, the theory of fraud, or that the body was stolen; second, that Jesus had not really died, but just fainted, and, when placed in the cool tomb, He revived. The

first theory had its origin back on the day of Christ's resurrection (Matt. 28:11-15). That was the only way the natural
mind could explain the empty tomb. We find no record anywhere where man has ever tried to disprove the empty tomb,
for that would have been an impossibility in the face of all
evidence. Therefore, they must either believe in the resurrection or resort to the theory that the body was stolen.

The first theory is incompatible with the life and conduct
of the Apostles (who were the supposed thieves) after His
resurrection. Certainly, if it had been a fraud, they would
never have been willing to die a martyr's death. According
to tradition, all of the apostles did, except John, who is supposed to have died a natural death, banished on the Isle of
Patmos for the sake of the gospel. Certainly not all of the
apostles would have been willing to display such heroism
just to cover up a fraud. This theory leaves too many problems unanswered.

In connection with the empty tomb, we have a good sum-
mary given by Evans, whom I quote: "The fact that the
tomb was empty is testified to by competent witnesses — both
friends and enemies: by the women, the disciples, the angels,
and the Roman guards. How shall we account for the absence of the body of Jesus from the tomb? That it had not
been stolen by outside parties is evident from the testimony
of the soldiers who were bribed to tell that story (Matt.
28:11-15). Such a guard never would have allowed such a
thing to take place. Their lives would have been thereby
jeopardized. And if they were asleep (v. 13), how could they
know what took place? Their testimony under such circumstances would be useless.

"The condition in which the linen cloths were found lying
by those who entered the tomb precludes the possibility of
the body being stolen. . . . Burglars do not leave things in
such perfect order. There is no order in haste."[13]

"The old theory of fraud on the part of the disciples has
no respectable advocate, and may be put out of account."[14]

---

13 *Ibid.*, page 87.
14 Orr, *op. cit.*, page 128.

We can only express our sincerest confidence in the Scriptural declaration that "He is risen."

The second theory mentioned above also rests on uncertain ground. Those who hold to the theory that Jesus just fainted or swooned, and that the people took pity on Him and removed Him from the cross before He died, hold that Jesus fooled His disciples.

The error of this theory is soon seen when reading the Gospel account. Just before Christ's death, He cried with a loud voice (Matt. 27:50), not as one half dead or one about to faint. When Christ appeared to the disciples the third day, He came to them, not as one that was weak or half dead, but rather as a triumphant victor or a conqueror.

The proof that He was actually dead is found in John 19:33-37, where it says that a soldier pierced His side, and "there came forth blood and water." (The previous chapter is given to the consideration of this miracle.) He was pronounced dead, as seen in the following accounts: "When even was come, there came a rich man of Arimathaea, named Joseph, who also himself was Jesus' disciple: he went to Pilate, and begged the body of Jesus. Then Pilate commanded the body to be delivered" (Matt. 27:57, 58). "And Pilate marvelled if he were already dead: and calling unto him the centurion, he asked him whether he had been any while dead. And when he knew it of the centurion, he gave the body to Joseph" (Mark 15:44, 45). "But when they came to Jesus, and saw that he was dead already, they brake not his legs" (John 19:33).

Jesus, Himself, after His resurrection, declared that He had actually been dead. "I am he that liveth, and was dead; and, behold, I am alive for evermore" (Rev. 1:18).

So, from the Gospel account and the testimony from the lips of the resurrected Christ, we see that He had actually died and had truly risen from the dead.

The other theory, which is generally used today to do away with this miracle, is the so-called "vision-hypothesis." This theory declares that the disciples did not actually see Jesus in His body, but that they just saw a vision of Him. This was supposedly due to their excited imagination, and the fact that they expected Jesus to rise from the dead. That such an event was not expected by the disciples is clearly stated by one of Christ's own disciples, when he explained how he came to believe in the resurrection of his Master. "For as yet they knew not the scripture, that he must rise again from the dead" (John 20:9). If the disciples were expecting Christ to rise from the dead the third day, it must be explained why it was that they were so fearful and so disappointed at His death.

Christ made certain that His disciples would never be tempted to believe that His appearance was only a spirit or a phantom, for He, in appearing to them, said (especially to Thomas), "Reach hither thy finger, and behold my hands; and reach hither thy hand, and thrust it into my side: and be not faithless, but believing" (John 20:27). Again, He said, "Behold my hands and my feet, that it is I myself: *handle me,* and see; for a spirit hath not flesh and bones, as ye see me have" (Luke 24:39). To further prove the reality of His resurrected body, He asked for something to eat (Luke 24:41-43), and He ate in their presence.

The adherents to the "vision-hypothesis" still have to explain the empty tomb. Who removed the body? Peter, some six weeks later, preached the resurrection of Christ at Jerusalem on the day of Pentecost, and we find that none dared silence him.

The only answer to the empty tomb is — HE IS RISEN!

WHAT WAS THE NATURE OF THE RESURRECTED BODY OF JESUS?

We have seen from Luke 24:36-39 that it was a real body, not just a ghost or a phantom. He had flesh and bones, and was visible. He bore the marks of His passion, for "He showed them his hands and his side" (John 20:20). We should remember that there are several other miracles listed in the Bible of people being raised to life. These, we know to have been bodily resurrections. From this we may well understand what is meant by the resurrection when it says that He arose.

Although it was a real body, it was, however, a changed body. The change in His body was "From one in which blood was the life to one in which the Spirit was the life."[15] For we read, "Christ also hath once suffered for sins, the just for the unjust, that he might bring us to God, being put to death in the flesh, but quickened [brought to life] by the Spirit" (I Peter 3:18). Although His body had flesh and bones, as He, Himself, declared, it did not have flesh and blood. The life of the natural body or flesh is in the blood, but the blood of Christ had been shed on the cross, and now He had come forth from the grave with a body without blood, but with flesh and bones, and the Spirit became the life of the resurrected body.

It is interesting to observe that when the eyes of the disciples were holden and they did not recognize Jesus, that He made Himself known to them at times by little acts, such as by the tone of His voice, or by breaking of bread, or just by the way He did things. We further observe that certain personal characteristics were carried over into the resurrected body. This proved that this was the *same* Jesus who had been crucified and raised from the dead.

There are evidences that His resurrected body had a relation to the celestial sphere. He was free from physical limitations, as, on "the first day of the week, when the doors were shut where the disciples were assembled for fear of the Jews, came Jesus and stood in the midst, and said unto them, Peace be unto you" (John 20:19). At times He also appeared in a form in which He was not recognizable. "And, behold, two of them went that same day to a village called Emmaus, which was from Jesusalem about threescore furlongs. And they talked together of all things which had happened. And it came to pass, that, while they communed together and reasoned, Jesus himself drew near, and went with them. But their eyes were holden that they should not know him"

---

15 Perry F. Haines, *The Jesus Paul Preached*, page 132.

(Luke 24:13-16). "And when she [Mary] had thus said, she turned herself back, and saw Jesus standing, and knew not that it was Jesus" (John 20:14). The disciples, in their discouragement, had gone fishing at night. "But when the morning was now come, Jesus stood on the shore: but the disciples knew not that it was Jesus" (John 21:4).

This shows that in His risen body, the spiritual controlled the material, instead of the material controlling the spiritual, as we experience in the natural body.

When Paul said that the eye has not seen, and even the imagination of man cannot comprehend the things God has prepared for His own, he said, "But God hath revealed them unto us by His Spirit" (I Cor. 2:10). In this Paul showed the close relationship of the mind and the spirit. "Thus, when the spirit and mind work together, the body will be able to obey every request and will of the mind, which, we believe, is seated in the spirit. As an example, we think of going to a distant place. In our mind we are there, but our body still remains just where we are while thinking. We must overcome our inability to propel our bodies through space by the help of some animal or mechanical device. That was not true of Jesus after His resurrection. His body was not limited by space or matter. We read in scientific books that mind is subject to matter, and we only need to try to walk through a stone wall to realize the accuracy of the statement. We repeat that in the case of Jesus in His resurrected body, the above fact seemed to be reversed, for matter was subject to His mind, as well as was space.... The body obeyed the mind and spirit.... In this immortal body of flesh and bones our Saviour, the Lord Jesus Christ, entered heaven to appear in the presence of God for all believers."[16]

The resurrected body of Jesus is also immortal — that is, since His resurrection, He cannot die again. This is clearly declared in the words of Paul as well as in the words of the risen Christ, Himself. "Knowing that Christ being raised from the dead dieth no more; death hath no more dominion

16 *Ibid.,* page 143, 144.

over him. For in that he died, he died unto sin once: but in
that he liveth, he liveth unto God" (Rom. 6:9, 10). "I am
he that liveth, and was dead, and, behold, I am alive for
evermore" (Rev. 1:18).

WHAT THIS MIRACLE TEACHES

So great a miracle must certainly have a special and significant teaching. What does it teach us? "One question still
remains. A meaningless miracle is incredible. Why, then,
should Jesus thus appear to His disciples in bodily form and
in such remarkable ways? He was desirous to convince them
that, despite the cross and the tomb, He was back with
them again, the same friend and guide and teacher, though
now the triumphant Lord of life and death. This fact was
so wonderful, so incredible, that it had to be taught in the
most unmistakable way. They must see Him as before: must
touch Him, talk with Him, walk with Him, eat with Him,
before they could feel that in very truth He was with them
of old."[17]

Thus, through His resurrection He is "declared to be the
Son of God with power" (Rom. 1:14). His resurrection declared His true relationship to the God-head. That which He
had claimed concerning Himself during the days of His
earthly life (John 14:10, 11) had now been unmistakably
demonstrated through His resurrection. He had proven that
He not only could lay down His life at His will, but that He
had power to take it up again (John 10:17, 18). The promised sign (Matt. 12:38-42; John 2:13-22) to prove that He
proceeded from the Father had been given in His resurrection. This is what He had tried to tell the disciples (Matt.
16:21), but they did not understand the truth that He was
going to rise until after the resurrection had taken place
(John 20:9; Luke 24:25, 26).

The resurrection declared, furthermore, that the sacrifice
on the cross had been acceptable to the Father. This was
partly taught in the lesson of the "Burnt-offering" in Leviti-

---

[17] Hill, *op. cit.*, page 55.

cus 1. The offering was for the Lord. We referred in a previous chapter to the day of Atonement for the Jews, as taught in Leviticus 16. Suffice it here to say that when the High Priest entered into the Holy of Holies with the blood sacrifice for the people, and then came forth from the presence of God to where the people were anxiously waiting, there was great rejoicing on the part of the people that the offering for their sins had been accepted. The return of the High Priest was the token of assurance that all was well.

Likewise, our Lord, who was not only the Sacrifice, but also the High Priest, offered Himself to God as a sacrifice for the sins of the world. On the third day God declared His approval and the acceptance of Christ's sacrifice by raising Jesus from the dead and had Him appear to the brethren. The resurrection of Jesus Christ from the dead is our *assurance* that the atonement was complete and satisfying to the Father, and now we are accepted in Him. He accepted the Son's sacrifice, and as we accept the Son we are accepted in Him. Faith in Him now justifies us in the sight of God. "He was delivered for our offences, and was raised again for our justification" (Rom. 4:25).

With this justification comes the assurance that we are kept by His power, for the power that raised Jesus from the dead is now resident in us. "But if the Spirit of him that raised up Jesus from the dead dwell in you, he that raised up Christ from the dead shall also quicken your mortal bodies by his Spirit that dwelleth in you" (Rom. 8:11). ". . . And what is the exceeding greatness of his power to us-ward who believe, according to the working of his mighty power, which he wrought in Christ, when he raised him from the dead, and set him at his own right hand in the heavenly places" (Eph. 1:19, 20). Paul wrote, "He which hath begun a good work in you will perform it until the day of Jesus Christ" (Phil. 1:6). This is only possible because the resurrected Christ has become our interceding High Priest (Heb. 7:25). Satan accuses us, but the Son is our Advocate (I John 2:1) on the ground of the shed blood and the triumphant resurrection.

The resurrection of Christ, further, teaches us that we, too, will be raised from the dead when He comes to take His own unto Himself. "For if we believe that Jesus died and rose again, even so them also which sleep in Jesus will God bring with him" (I Thess. 4:14). "Knowing that he which raised up the Lord Jesus shall raise up us also by Jesus, and shall present us with you" (II Cor. 4:14). In the resurrection we will be given a body like unto the glorious body of Jesus Christ. In this body the Spirit and not the blood will be the life. When we dealt with the nature of the resurrected body of Jesus, we saw that His resurrected body was such. So, in our resurrection our bodies will be like unto His. "We shall be like him, for we shall see him as he is" (I John 3:2). Christ was the "first-fruits of them that slept" (I Cor. 15:20). This term is taken from the Old Testament feast as recorded in Leviticus 23. In verses 10 and 11 we have the feast of the "first-fruits." Giving the first grain to the Lord guaranteed them the remainder of the harvest. Christ's resurrection, the first-fruits, guarantees the resurrection of all believers. Since the remainder of the harvest was the same kind of grain as the first-fruits, we, therefore, must conclude that the bodies of all believers will be like Christ's own resurrected body.

It will be a spiritual body. "It is sown a natural body, it is raised a spiritual body" (I Cor. 15:44). This does not mean that the composition of the body will be spiritual or non-material, but rather that it will be a body motivated and controlled by the Spirit. This body, like the body of Jesus, will not be limited by the natural surroundings. It, too, will overcome the material barriers and be made fit to live in the presence of God. It will be, as we learn from the words of Paul, a glorified body. "For our conversation is in heaven; from whence also we look for the Saviour, the Lord Jesus Christ: Who shall *change our vile body,* that it may be fashioned like unto his glorious body, according to the working whereby he is able even to subdue all things unto himself" (Phil. 3:20, 21).

The resurrection of Jesus Christ, also, carries with it a message of warning. Because He arose from the dead, the ungodly, too, will be raised from the dead. "As in Adam all die; even so in Christ shall *all be made alive*" (I Cor. 15:22). This *all* also includes all those who have died without Christ. Not only will those who have done good be raised, but all "those that have done evil, unto the resurrection of damnation" (John 5:29).

This is further confirmed in the book of Acts, where the Apostle Paul on Mar's hill warned the people to repent, "because he [God] hath appointed a day, in the which he will judge the world in righteousness by that man whom he hath ordained; whereof he hath given assurance unto all men, in that he hath raised him from the dead" (Acts 17:31). "The resurrection of Christ is God's unfailing testimony to the fact of a coming day of judgment for the world."[18]

Let us never think lightly about the resurrection of Jesus Christ. Upon our faith in this glorious miracle hinges our eternal destiny.

> "The strife is o'er, the battle done,
> The victory of life is won;
> The song of triumph has begun.
> Alleluia!

> "The powers of death have done their worst,
> But Christ their legions hath dispersed:
> Let shout of holy joy out-burst.
> Alleluia!

> "The three sad days are quickly sped,
> He rises glorious from the dead:
> All glory to our risen Head!
> Alleluia!

> "He closed the yawning gates of hell,
> The bars from heaven's high portals fell,
> Let hymns of praise His triumphs tell!
> Alleluia!"
>   — Giovanni Palestrina

---

18 Evans. *op. cit.*, page 96.

6. The Undisturbed Grave Clothes at Christ's Resurrection

When Christ had dismissed His Spirit, and in fulfilment of prophesy, the Roman soldier had pierced His side, all things were fulfilled. The body of Jesus was then ready to be removed from the cross. Concerning this we read, "After this Joseph of Arimathaea, being a disciple of Jesus, but secretly for fear of the Jews, besought Pilate that he might take away the body of Jesus: and Pilate gave him leave. He came therefore, and took the body of Jesus. And there came also Nicodemus, which at the first came to Jesus by night, and brought a mixture of myrrh and aloes, about an hundred pound weight. Then took they the body of Jesus, and wound it in linen clothes with the spices, as the manner of the Jews is to bury. Now in the place where He was crucified there was a garden; and in the garden a new sepulchre, wherein was never man yet laid. There laid they Jesus therefore because of the Jews' preparation day; for the sepulchre was nigh at hand" (John 19:38-42).

THE BURIAL

Immediate burial of the dead was deemed urgent by the Jewish people. There was a general fear of defilement by contact with a dead body which would certainly occasion such urgency. "It was in strict accordance with such customs and the provision of the Mosaic Law ['And if a man have committed a sin worthy of death, and he be to be put to death, and thou hang him on a tree: his body shall not remain all night upon the tree, but thou shalt in any wise bury him that day; (for he that is hanged is accursed of God) that thy land be not defiled, which the Lord thy God giveth thee for an inheritance' (Deut. 21:22, 23)] as well as in compliance with the impulses of true humanity, that Joseph of Arimathea went to Pilate and begged the body of Jesus for burial on the very day of the crucifixion."[1]

It is evident that the burial of Christ was done in compliance with the ordinary Jewish practice, in which "linen bandages were wound around the body and limbs, the mixture of myrrh and aloes was strewn in. That was the manner in which the Jews prepared their dead for burial."[2] The head, however, would be wound about with a separate bandage or what was known as the head napkin. Thus, the body would be placed in the family tomb.

The graves were excavations in rocky cliffs, with rooms for burial, as indicated in a previous chapter. Often there would be family caves, that is, there would be large rooms cut out in the rocky cliff, and in these rooms burial vaults would be excavated along the walls for as many as were in the family. When it speaks of Joseph of Arimathea's tomb, "wherein was never man yet laid" (John 19:41), it means that none of the burial vaults in his family tomb had been used — it was still entirely empty. It was in such a tomb that Jesus was laid.

In Jewish custom, "when the tomb was a cave, or was dug out from some rock, the entrance was often closed with a large circular stone set up on its edge or rim and rolled in its groove to the front of the mouth of the tomb, so as to close it securely. This stone was then often further secured by a strap, or by sealing. In such a case it could easily be seen or known if the tomb had been disturbed. Pilate, it will be recalled, directed that the tomb of Joseph of Arimathea, in which the body of Jesus was laid, should be carefully sealed, and made as secure as the officials could make it. 'So

---

[1] *International Standard Bible Encyclopedia,* Vol. 1, page 529.
[2] Wm. Hendriksen, *New Testament Commentary on the Gospel of John,* Vol. II, page 442.

they went, and made the sepulchre sure, sealing the stone, the guard being with them' (Matt. 27:66) ."[3]

Thus, the body of Jesus was properly buried, according to Jewish custom, but under the guard of the Roman government.

THE TWO BURIALS

It is frequently overlooked that Jesus had two burials instead of just one. One was just a hurried affair, and the other was a more permanent burial, according to Jewish custom. This truth comes to us by a close observation of the Gospel narratives.

There are two reasons for concluding that Christ had two burials, although there might have been only a brief time that elapsed between the two. The first reason is because of the order of events as recorded by Luke and John. The next reason is because of the Greek words used to describe the burial garments used in each case.

First of all, let us look at the order of events as recorded by Luke and John. The hurried burial is given to us in Luke 23:50-56. The final burial, which was according to Jewish custom, is recorded in John 19:39-42. After Joseph of Arimathea had gained consent from Pilate (which agrees with John 19:38), he took the body from the cross, "and wrapped it in linen, and laid it in a sepulchre that was hewn in stone" (Luke 23:53).

John 19:39-41 records for us the regular burial following the hasty removal of the body from the cross. Then it must have been that Joseph of Arimathea got together with Nicodemus. We read, "There came also Nicodemus, which at the first came to Jesus by night, and brought a mixture of myrrh and aloes, about an hundred pound weight. Then took they the body of Jesus, and wound it in linen clothes with the spices, as the manner of the Jews is to bury" (John 19:39, 40). The first burial was just a hasty removal of the body

---

[3] *Ibid.,* page 531.

from the cross, but Nicodemus joined Joseph of Arimathea for the true Jewish burial.

In Luke's account we read, "And the women also, which came with Him from Galilee, followed after, and beheld the sepulchre, and *how His body was laid*. And they returned, and prepared spices and ointments; and rested the sabbath day according to the commandment" (Luke 23:55, 56). It was when they had observed that He had not been buried according to Jewish custom, that they went home and prepared those spices for the proper burial, which they brought to the grave on the first day of the week. If the burial which they observed had been complete, according to Jewish tradition, as John 19 gives it to us, there would have been no point in their coming to the grave.

Having seen the Gospel narrative concerning this, let us also look at the Greek words employed to show the difference. Dr. Perry F. Haines, in his book, *The Jesus Paul Preached,* in Chapter 11, confirmed this very same thing upon the usage of the Greek words.

Let us go back again to Luke 23:50-56 where it is said that Joseph took the body, "and wrapped it in linen." The Greek word here for linen is SINDON; meaning a fine linen garment or wrap used as a sleeping garment. This same word is used in Mark 14:50-52, where we read, "And they all forsook Him and fled, and there followed Him a certain young man, having a linen cloth (SINDON) cast about his naked body; and the young men laid hold on him: and he left the linen cloth (SINDON) and fled from them naked." The linen in which Jesus was first buried, then, was just a loose linen garment or wrap. This was not intended to be a permanent burial, but just a hasty removal from the place of execution.

In John 19:38-42 we have an entirely different word used for the grave clothes. Here the Greek word is OTHONION, meaning linen bandages. John said that the body was now wound (according to Jewish custom) in linen cloths. It is remarkable that when Luke wrote about Joseph of Arimathea burying the body of Jesus, he said that he "wrapped Him in linen (SINDON)" (Luke 23:53), but in writing about the empty tomb, he said that "the linen clothes (OTHONION) laid by themselves" (Luke 24:12).

With the Gospel narrative giving us the order of events and with the two different Greek words for the burial garments, we have indicated for us that there were actually two burials. The first burial was a hasty removal of the body of Jesus from the cross. It was placed in the sepulchre that belonged to the man who had asked for His body, Joseph of Arimathea. Following this, he, together with Nicodemus, gave the body of the Lord the proper Jewish burial, and rolled the stone in front of the open tomb.

The understanding of the mode of Jewish burial, and of the grave clothes with which the body was finally laid away, will help us to understand what Peter and John saw when they entered the tomb. "The first day of the week cometh Mary Magdalene early, when it was yet dark, unto the sepulchre, and seeth the stone taken away from the sepulchre. Then she runneth, and cometh to Simon Peter, and to the other disciple, whom Jesus loved, and saith unto them. They have taken away the Lord out of the sepulchre, and we know not where they have laid him. Peter therefore went forth, and that other disciple, and came to the sepulchre. So they ran both together: and the other disciple did outrun Peter, and came first to the sepulchre. And he stooping down, and looking in, saw the linen clothes lying; yet went he not in. Then cometh Simon Peter following him, and went into the sepulchre, and seeth the linen clothes lie, and the napkin, that was about his head, not lying with the linen clothes, but wrapped together in a place by itself. Then went in also that other disciple, which came first to the sepulchre, and he saw, and believed. For as yet they knew not the scripture, that he must rise again from the dead" (John 20:1-9).

We now enter upon a study of what John saw when he entered the tomb, and what it was that made him suddenly believe in the physical resurrection of the crucified and buried Jesus. Let me introduce this consideration with the following quotation. In the above description given by

John (20:1-9) "we have a very strong proof for the bodily resurrection of Jesus. When John saw the linen clothes, OTHONIA or burial bandages, lying there with no body in them, he could not but believe in a bodily resurrection. We are convinced that the burial bandages were seen lying in their original convolutions as when they had enveloped the arms, legs and trunk of Jesus."[4]

VARYING VIEWS

We used the above paragraph as a steppingstone to bring to your attention some of the prevailing views concerning what Peter and John saw in the sepulchre. Let me bring to your attention, first of all, some of the arguments which are given against the above view.

Hendriksen said, "Ideas such as these, namely, that the head band was lying there as if it had not been removed from the head, and that the bandages were lying there just as if the limbs of Jesus were still enclosed by them, or as if the body had been abstracted from them, are foreign to the text. . . . What Luke emphasizes is that the bandages were lying there by *themselves,* which, again, does not mean that they were being held in position mysteriously and in violation to the laws of gravity; but simply indicates that they were lying there *without* the body."[5] He thought that the orderliness was to indicate resurrection. To this Bengel added, "Doubtless, the two attendant angels did this service for the Risen One; the one disposed of the linen clothes and the other of the napkin."[6] Some think that the laying aside and the folding of the bandages must have been an act of Christ, Himself, — but that it was not done in any hurry.[7] Wescott seemingly would agree with this when he wrote, "The grave clothes had been carefully removed, which would

---

4 Haines, *op. cit.,* pages 123, 124.
5 Hendriksen, *op. cit.,* page 450.
6 Quoted by Jamieson, Fausset and Brown, *op. cit.,* page 478.
7 *Ibid,* page 478.

be a work of time and difficulty, and laid in two separate places."[8]

There are those who think that the orderliness of the grave and of the grave clothes is what bears witness to the resurrection. "Observe, too, the further witness of the folded grave clothes. John, from outside, had not seen the napkin, lying carefully rolled up. . . . But the careful disposal of these came to him when he saw with a great flash of illumination. There had been no hurried removal."[9] To this we would add the following: "There is no suggestion that the wrappings of the body have been hastily torn off by thieves; on the contrary, there is the impression of leisure, as if they had been carefully removed."[10]

To my understanding, these conclusions would not be sufficient proof of Christ's resurrection. There was something in particular that these two disciples observed which caused them to suddenly believe in the resurrection.

WHAT AND *HOW* THEY SAW

John, in writing this account, did not only speak of *what* they saw, but he pointed out *how* three different people saw. He said (John 20:1-9) concerning Mary Magdalene, as she came to the sepulchre, she "*seeth* the stone taken away from the sepulchre" (v. 1) . John ran ahead of Peter to the sepulchre and, "he stooping down, and looking in, *saw* the linen clothes lying. Then cometh Simon Peter following him, and went into the sepulchre, and *seeth* the linen clothes lie. . . ." (vv. 5, 6) . After this, "went in also that other disciple [John], . . . and he *saw*, and believed" (v. 8) .

When Mary Magdalene came to the tomb, she simply "seeth (BLEPO) the stone taken away." BLEPO means to see in the ordinary sense of the word. When John arrived ahead of Peter and stooped to look in, he simply "saw (BLEPO) the linen clothes lying." Here, too, it is just the

---

8 *Op. cit.*
9 Alexander Maclaren, *Exposition of Holy Scriptures*, Vol. 7, page 303.
10 George Appleton, *John's Witness to Jesus*, page 88.

thought of seeing without any sense of seeing with understanding. It just passed across his vision. But when Peter looked, it says that he "seeth (THEOREO) the linen clothes." THEOREO means more than to just see, but it has the thought of seeing as a spectator, to look critically and carefully upon the surroundings. When John entered, an entirely different word from the above two Greek words was used to express what and how he saw. "He saw (EIDO), and believed." EIDO has the meaning of understanding, to know or to be sure. John looked with understanding. This had real meaning to him. He was convinced that Jesus was risen from the dead. To this agreed McCaulay.[11]

The question constantly arises, "What was it that led to this sudden belief that Christ was risen from the dead?" John wrote, "for as yet they knew not the scripture, that he must rise again from the dead" (John 20:9). They did not look for His resurrection. "It was not the belief previously derived from Scripture, that the Christ was to rise from the dead, which led to expectancy of it, but the evidence that He had risen led them to the knowledge of what Scripture taught on the subject."[12]

Mary saw the stone rolled away. This led her to the conclusion that the body had been stolen. When John arrived ahead of Peter, he saw more than Mary. He looked in and saw the grave clothes.

A good bit of discussion and speculation have been ventured by various authors as to why John did not go ahead of Peter into the tomb, since he outran him. Some feel that John saw enough to satisfy his curiosity when he looked in from the outside. But notice, when Peter came and entered, John went in, too. I believe Lenski was right when he attributed it to "psychological differences between John's personality and that of Peter.... It is what John sees from the entrance that rivets his feet."[13]

---

11 J. C. McCaulay, *Devotional Studies in St. John's Gospel*, page 268.
12 Edersheim, *op. cit.*, page 634.
13 *Op. cit.*, page 1341.

What did they see in the tomb? "The linen clothes lying
..." (John 20:5, 6). They saw the "grave clothes as they had
been wound about the body of Jesus, with all the spices in
the windings, undisturbed;... They were not unwound."[14]
"We are not to imagine that they had been unwound from
the body as was done with the grave clothes of Lazarus when
he came to life. Neither had they been cut or stripped off in
some other way. They lay just as they had been wound about
the limbs and body, only the body was no longer in them,
and thus the wrappings lay flat. All the aromatic spices were
exactly as they had been strewn between the layers of linen,
and these layers, one wound over the other, were numerous,
so that all those spices could be held between them.... No
human being, wrapped round and round with bands like
that, could possibly slip out of them without greatly disturbing them. They would have to be unwound, or cut through
or cut and stripped off. That is what would have been done
with the linen if hostile hands had handled it. Or if stolen,
grave clothes would have been taken. But here the linen
bands were. Both their presence and their undisturbed condition spoke volumes."[15] As Haines put it, "The man-made
cocoon was still there, but the heavenly butterfly had
flown."[16] It was the position of the grave clothes that "made
the disciples leap to the conclusion that the material body
had been transformed into a spiritual body."[17]

In this portion of scripture (John 20:1-9), "The whole
language seems to have been carefully chosen to suggest that
Jesus' physical body had passed into a spiritual and 'glorified' risen body without disturbing the grave clothes, which
had simply settled down on the ledge within the tomb in
their original position."[18] Thus, from all indications, the
grave clothes lay there, even as they had been wound about
the body and limbs of Jesus.

---

14 Morgan, pages 309, 310.
15 Lenski, *op. cit.*, page 1341.
16 *Op. cit.*, page 125.
17 *The Interpreter's Bible*, on Luke and John, page 790.
18 *The Moffatt New Testament Commentary*, page 356.

THE HEAD CLOTH

But, as important as the arrangement of the grave bandages was, there seems to be a special significance attached to the napkin that had been wound about His head. "The napkin, that was about His head, not lying with the linen clothes, but wrapped together in a place by itself" (v. 7).

Writers are not all agreed as to what is meant by the statement, "wrapped together in a place by itself." Because the head was generally wrapped separately, that is, with a napkin instead of with the bandages, some feel that when it says, "wrapped together" that it means that the napkin had been taken into the hands of the risen Lord, and folded, thus giving another witness for His resurrection. Here, let me quote Lenski. "The napkin [head cloth] which had been on the head of Jesus, lay in a place apart from the wrappings, neatly folded up, or we may say, rolled up. It had been done purposely by hands as the perfect participle indicates.

"One may ask why Jesus had not left the cloth as He did the bands, simply passing out of it and leaving its fastenings undisturbed; for that, too, would have been an eloquent sign. One answer is that then both the clothes and the bands would have uttered the same testimony; then Jesus would have left but one witness. He left two (Matt. 18:16) ."[19]

I, personally, cannot see how it would in any way intensify the resurrection evidence by placing the napkin apart in a separate corner or location in the tomb. It would seem more consistent with the whole picture to take the view that the head napkin had simply fallen together in its folds as it had been twirled turban-like about His head, thus revealing that the man-made cocoon was empty — that its occupant had moved out.

That John places special emphasis on the napkin is evident. Morgan said, "The most significant statement is that the napkin lay by itself, separately and that it was still in the folds as it had been about the head of Jesus. . . .

"Into those rock-hewn tombs the body was carried and laid,

---

[19] *Op. cit.,* page 1341.

the feet toward the opening, and the head further in, the body lay on the stone ledge; upon which ledge there was a slight elevated place for the head. The napkin about the head was thus always separate from the wrappings about the body. When Peter looked, he saw the grave clothes lying. John had seen that, but that fact had no particular significance for him. . . . Moreover the napkin, wrapped in a peculiar way about the head, was undisturbed, 'folded up.' That word does not mean smoothed out. The napkin was still in the folds that had been wound round the head. . . ."[20]

The whole picture seems to settle into focus. What Peter, and especially John, saw in the tomb, though at first somewhat dimly due to the darkness in the tomb, was that the bandages with which Jesus had been so lovingly wrapped, were there, all in order, but the occupant was gone. At a glance, from the outside, it would appear that He was still there, but upon entering, and with close scrutiny, it was found that "it was impossible that He should be holden of death." Death had no power over Him. The wrappings with the myrrh and aloes were there. The napkin, in its peculiar twirl, was there possibly on the headrest, fallen together in its original folds, *revealing that the bandages were truly empty.*

Thus, when John and Peter came they were "compelled to believe in a bodily resurrection, for the body was gone. Men did not take it as proved by the banadges being still there in the original folds. Had they been unwound and lying on the floor, that would have shown human tampering and that would not have convinced John that Jesus had risen from the dead."[21]

THE PROMISED "SIGN" GIVEN

The *sign* that Jesus had promised to the unbelieving enemies during the days of His early ministry had finally been given. The empty tomb, with its empty bandages, is the

[20] *Op. cit.,* page 310.
[21] Haines, *op. cit.,* page 125.

strongest proof of His Deity and of all that He claimed to be.

Again and again the skeptics of Christ's day had been asking for a sign — proof that He was the Son of God. At the time that Christ, in the second chapter of John, cleansed the temple, poured out the changers' money, overthrew their tables and drove them all out, they came to Him and said, "What sign shewest thou unto us, seeing that thou doest these things? Jesus answered and said unto them, Destroy this temple and in three days I will raise it up. But he spake of the temple of his body" (John 2:18, 19, 21). This saying was thrown back at Christ at least twice by His enemies. Once when Christ was standing before Caiaphas and the Sanhedrin, they said, "This fellow said, I am able to destroy the temple of God, and build it in three days" (Matt. 26:61). Then again, when He was hanging on the cross in all the agony, the people said, "Thou that destroyest the temple, and buildest it in three days, save thyself" (Matt. 27:40). This certainly indicates that they did not understand the true meaning of the sign when He said, "Destroy this temple and in three days I will raise it up." His resurrection was to be the *sign*.

On another occasion, in the early part of Christ's earthly ministry among men, the Pharisees and scribes came to Jesus and said, "Master, we would see a sign [token of proof] from thee. But he answered and said unto them, An evil and adulterous generation seeketh after a sign; and there shall no sign be given to it, but the sign of the prophet Jonas" (Matt. 12:38, 39). Again, at a later time, the Pharisees came to Jesus and desired a sign from heaven. Hear the words of Jesus, "A wicked and adulterous generation seeketh after a sign; and there shall no sign be given unto it, but the sign of Jonas" (Matt. 16:4).

Jesus declared that there would be only one sign given to the unbelieving world, and that would be the sign of Jonah, or as Christ, Himself, interpreted in Matthew 12:40, the sign of His bodily resurrection from the grave on the third day.

The sign was given. Christ arose from the dead triumphantly. But what did the unbelieving Jews do with this truth? They still would not believe, proving the truth of the words of Jesus when He said, "If they hear not Moses and the prophets, neither will they be persuaded, though one rose from the dead" (Luke 16:31).

The Pharisees still refused to believe, though in fulfilment of the promise of Christ, the sign which He had declared had been given.

In order to see the wickedness of the sin-bent, unbelieving heart, let me quote at length what men did with this heaven-sent sign. "Now the next day, that followed the day of preparation, the chief priests and Pharisees came together unto Pilate, saying, Sir, we remember that that deceiver said, while he was yet alive, After three days I will rise again. Command therefore that the sepulchre be made sure until the third day, lest his disciples come by night, and steal him away, and say unto the people, he is risen from the dead: so the last error shall be worse than the first. Pilate said unto them, Ye have a watch: go your way, make it as sure as ye can. So they went, and made the sepulchre sure, sealing the stone, and setting a watch. And, behold, there was a great earthquake: for the angel of the Lord descended from heaven, and came and rolled back the stone from the door, and sat upon it. His countenance was like lightning, and his raiment white as snow: And for fear of him the keepers did shake, and become as dead men. Now when they were going, behold, some of the watch came into the city, and shewed unto the chief priests all the things that were done. And when they were assembled with the elders, and had taken counsel, they gave large money unto the soldiers, Saying, Say ye, His disciple came by night, and stole him away while we slept. And if this come to the governor's ears, we will persuade him, and secure you. So they took the money, and did as they were taught: and this saying is commonly reported among the Jews until this day" (Matt. 27:62-66; 28:2-4, 11-15).

It is very possible that John included the account we have in Chapter 20:1-9 to disprove this false notion of the people as given in Matthew 28:13. It is quite probable that the error, that the body of Jesus had been stolen, was widespread during the days that John wrote this account. According to all indications, John wrote his Gospel narrative some fifty years after Matthew wrote. Thus, the common report that the body was stolen could have been propagated quite extensively. Because of this, I believe that John was constrained to give us an eyewitness report of the condition of the grave, which would disprove any notion that an enemy had tampered with the body.

"Look, ye saints, the sight is glorious, See the Man of Sorrows now;
From the fight returned victorious, Every knee to Him shall bow:
   Crown Him, crown Him! Crown Him, crown Him!
   Crowns become the Victor's brow.

"Hark, those bursts of acclamation! Hark, those loud triumphant chords!
Jesus takes the highest station: O what joy the sight affords!
   Crown Him, crown Him! Crown Him, crown Him!
   King of kings, and Lord of lords!"
                                        — Thomas Kelly

7. Revival to Life of Departed Saints

The final miracle that occurred on Golgotha's Hill in connection with the Lord's death is given to us by Matthew in these words: "And many bodies of the saints which slept arose, and came out of the graves after his resurrection, and appeared unto many" (Matt. 27:52, 53).

This brief declaration by Matthew has by no means been exempt from the attacks of the critics. There are those who hold that the symbolic fact of the graves that were opened by the earthquake at the time of Christ's death caused the injection into the traditional history the teaching that certain persons actually arose from the graves. They, therefore, declare the passage to be an "aprocryphal and mythical supplement."[1] Others, regarding the "... opening of the graves, and appearing of many bodies of the saints, as Norton, have rejected it as an interpolation."[2]

There is, however, no ground to doubt the authenticity of this brief but tremendous statement by Matthew. In fact, historians have stated that "Matthew was probably an eye-witness of that which he relates, and might have been confuted by his contemporaries, if he had stated what was not true. An early witness to the fact is found in Ignatius, who, in his Epistle to the Magnesians, ch. ix, speaks of Christ when on earth raising the prophets from the dead."[3]

Lange adds another note, which is worthy of quoting, although there might be some question as to whether or not the statement can be fully substantiated. I could not find his authority for the following quotation, but I give it for

---

[1] Meyer's view quoted in *Lange's Commentary on Matthew*, page 527.
[2] Samuel Andrews, *The Life of Our Lord Jesus*, page 546.
[3] *Pulpit Commentary on Matthew*, Vol. 2, pages 595-596.

what it may be worth. "In a circle of living people, which was equally friendly to the saintly dead and to the living Evangelist, several men contemporaneously, after the resurrection of Christ, related that the spirits of pious dead people appeared to them. These appearances had the peculiarity, that they were so frequent — that the risen saints appeared to many. In that case, they represented themselves to those who saw them in the dawn of the new life of corporeality."[4]

When we regard this, as we do the other events connected with the death of Christ, as a miracle, it is not so difficult for us to accept as a reality the resurrection of the saints at that time. The miraculous is seen in that not all of the saints arose, but that a certain large number of the bodies came forth from the graves. This proves the presence of the hand of God. God was in it. Therefore, without any further doubt, we can accept the accuracy of the Biblical statement.

To prove the reality of their resurrection, it says that they appeared to many. Regarding this, Bishop Nicholson said, "Indeed, the thought in the text is not merely that they 'appeared' — which does not fully express the original — but that they were manifestly made known. It is not said that they were made known as to their names. The only thing implied is, that they were manifestly made known as persons risen from the dead."[5] So we see that it was not only that they appeared, but that they left no doubt in the minds of those with whom they came into contact that they were truly dead people raised to life again.

Some hold that these saints arose from the dead at the time of Christ's death, but appeared to the people after Christ's resurrection. Prat contended thus, "One would be tempted to establish a link of causality between the two phenomena; but there is none; since the opening of the tombs occurred after the resurrection of Jesus. St. Jerome thinks that the tombs were opened at the time of the earthquake, and perhaps as an effect of it, but that the dead did not come forth until after Christ's resurrection. It is better to say with

---

[4] Lange, *op. cit.*, page 324.
[5] *Op. cit.*, page 112.

Maldonatus, that the opening of the tombs, as well as the coming forth of their occupants, is mentioned here by antici-pation."[6] To this Andrews said, "It was the Lord's resurrec-tion, not death, that opened the gates of Hades. Dying, the rocks were rent, and the doors of the sepulchres were opened; but, rising, He gave life to the dead."[7] This view is also confirmed by Calvin, Lightfoot, A. Clarke, Bengel, Alford and others. Lange, also, is of the conviction that these resur-rections mentioned did not take place until after Christ's resurrection. Upon a closer examination of this account by Matthew, we realize that, "The rising was the result, not the immediate accomplishment of the opening of the graves, and is mentioned here by Matthew in anticipation, but with qualifying insertion, *after His resurrection,* to prevent misun-derstanding. Christ's death opened their tombs, His resur-rection raised them to life again, that He might be the first-born from the dead, and the first-fruits of them that slept."[8]

Our faith need not falter here. We have here the sure Word of God to stand good for what is declared. The miracu-lous calls for faith, not for a natural explanation. "By faith we understand" (Heb. 11:3). This event "harmonizes with and explains the wonder of the open graves, just as that won-der was the product of the wondrous earthquake, and the earthquake was the counterpart of the wondrous rending of the veil, which rending of the veil answered back to the shout of victory from the cross whose dying Sufferer had just emerged in triumph out of the almighty horrors of the sym-bolic darkness! So, if that line of Calvary's wonders is his-torical, then, by a harmonic necessity this is the only con-ceivable conclusion of the great series."[9]

WHO WERE THE SAINTS THAT AROSE?

As one reads the brief account by Matthew, there crowd into our minds numerous questions, such as: Who were these

---

[6] *Op. cit.,* page 398.
[7] *Op cit.,* page 547.
[8] *Op. cit.,* page 528.
[9] Nicholson, *op. cit.,* pages 109, 110.

saints? How many were there that came forth from the grave? When had they died? How long were they in the Holy City after their resurrection? What effect did this have on the people who saw them? These and other questions present themselves.

The Scripture seems to be silent on this. Matthew just gives us the brief statement, "Many bodies of the saints which slept arose, and came out of the graves after his resurrection, and went into the holy city, and appeared unto many" (Matt. 27:52, 53). As far as identity is concerned, all we know is that they were saints. However, the fact "that those who arose are called 'saints', AGIOI, does not determine who are meant; whether some who had died recently, perhaps since Christ began His ministry, or some who died long before, and had been buried there."[10] Plummer says that the "expression (saints, AGIOI) is found nowhere else in the Gospels; and elsewhere in the New Testament is found always of Christians (see Acts 9:13, 41; 12:13; 15:25, 26, 31, etc.) ."[11] From this, one would conclude that the saints that arose were those who had, in their lifetime, looked for the coming of the Messiah, who would be their redemption.

There is quite a difference of opinion as to what era of history to place these saints. It might seem like a waste of space to compare the opinions of various authors regarding this. However, I believe it is very interesting to make a few comparisons.

Barnes said, "It is probable that they were persons who had recently died, and they appeared to have been known in Jerusalem; at least, had the ancient saints risen, they would not so soon have been credited as those who had recently died."[12] Plummer contended that since they were saints, and the expression is used elsewhere in the New Testament only of believers, as mentioned above, he wrote. "It would seem therefore, to mean those who, *like* Simeon

---

[10] Andrews, *op. cit.*, page 546.
[11] *An Exegetical Commentary on the Gospel According to Saint Matthew*, page 403.
[12] *Barnes' Notes on Matthew*, page 314.

and Anna, Zacharias and Elizabeth, had accepted Jesus as the Messiah."[13] Another writer indicated that "the Jews probably would have understood the term to apply to the worthies of the Old Testament. But the opening of the sepulchres in the neighborhood of Jerusalem would not have liberated the bodies of many of those who were buried far away. The persons signified must be those who in life had looked for the hope of Israel, and had seen in Christ that hope fulfilled."[14]

Schaff wrote, "There is also a difference of opinion among commentaries as to the question whether they were patriarchs and other saints of the olden times to whom Jerusalem was indeed a *Holy* City, or saints who lately died and were personally known to some of the living. Owen favors the latter opinion with a doubtful 'doubtless,' and specifies Simeon, Hannah and Zechariah. Dr. Nast adds John the Baptist and Joseph. But in the absence of all Scriptural information, it is perfectly useless to speculate on the age and number of these mysterious visitors from the spirit world. So much only appears certain to us, that it was a supernatural and symbolic event which proclaimed the truth that the death and resurrection of Christ was a victory over death and Hades, and opened the doors to everlasting life."[15]

Perhaps the reason that the Lord saw fit to withhold the names of these resurrected saints was to keep men, in the days that followed, from making them objects of worship, as man is so prone to do. Christ is the center of our worship. Who the resurrected saints were has nothing to do with our salvation. But, whether or not Christ actually arose does determine the authenticity of our faith. "If Christ be not raised, your faith is vain; ye are yet in your sins" (I Cor. 15:17). Prat also feels that to hazard their names (as St. Joseph, St. John the Baptist, the Good Thief) would be empty conjecture.

We are not told how many there were, but simply that

---

[13] *Op. cit.*, page 403.
[14] *Pulpit Commentary on Matthew*, Vol. 2, page 595, 596.
[15] In a footnote in *Lange's Commentary on Matthew*, page 528.

many bodies arose. There were *enough* to vindicate the resurrection of Christ, and also to indicate that their resurrection was real. It was a true witness. As to how long they remained in the Holy City, the account is entirely silent. They were there long enough to appear to many. Whether they appeared only to believers, or to the unbelieving multitude also remains unanswered. Only believers are recorded to have seen Jesus after His resurrection. May we not from this, possibly also, draw the conclusion that these saints presented themselves only to the believers?

WHAT KIND OF RESURRECTION WAS THEIRS?

This calls to our attention the question, With what kind of body did these saints come forth from the grave? There are listed for us in the Bible six other resurrections that occurred previous to the day Christ arose. These were restorations to the natural physical life. They were: the son of the widow of Zarephath (I Kings 17), the son of the Shunammite woman (II Kings 4), the man who revived and stood upon his feet when his dead body touched the bones of Elisha (II Kings 13), the daughter of Jairus (Matt. 9), the son of the widow of Nain (Luke 17), and Lazarus, the brother of Mary and Martha (John 11). These were just revivals of the natural body, which were by no means glorified bodies like unto the body with which Jesus came forth out of His borrowed tomb. The question is, did these saints, who came forth from the grave the day Christ arose, each come forth with such a body as the above mentioned six people, or did they come out in their glorified resurrected state, such as *all* saints will have at the great resurrection.

Here, also, we find that Bible scholars are not fully in agreement. Spurgeon, though not too clearly stated, seems to lean toward the theory that those who arose came forth in the final and glorified bodies, for he said, "They were representative men; they arose as specimens of the way in which all saints shall in due time arise."[16] His statement that they

---

16 *The Biblical Illustrator,* on Matthew, page 662.

were specimen of the way all saints shall arise infers that he thought that they arose with the glorified bodies. Another writes, "It must be observed, however, that the resurrection of these sleeping saints *was not* like those of the widow of Nain's son, of Jairus' daughter, of Lazarus, and the man who 'revived, and stood up on his feet' his dead body touching the bones of Elisha (II Kings 13:21) — which were mere temporary recallings of the departed spirits to the mortal body, to be followed by a final departure of it 'till the trump shall sound.' But this was a resurrection *once for all to life* everlasting."[17]

Edersheim does not express dogmatically his exact position regarding this. He wrote: "Does it mean that they were actually clothed with the resurrection-body, or with the body which they had formerly borne, or that many saints from Hades appeared to those who loved them, and with them had waited for the Kingdom, in the forms which they had known? We know too little of the connection between the other world and this, and the mode in which the departed may communicate with those here, to venture on any decided statement, especially as we take into account the unique circumstances of the occasion."[18]

I am inclined to agree with those who believe that the saints arose with their natural bodies. Theirs were not the true resurrected, glorified bodies. "They were not mere phantoms, unsubstantial visitants from the spirit-world, for they were in some sense corporeal. That they were resuscitated corpses, as Lazarus, Jairus' daughter, and the son of the widow, who lived for a time a second life, seems plain from the expression applied to them in the next verse (53), that 'they appeared unto many,' i.e. to persons who had known them while living."[19]

I believe that Scripture bears out this last view, though possibly not directly stated in the account given to us by Matthew. In I Corinthians 15, the great resurrection chapter,

---

[17] Jamieson, Fausett and Brown, *op. cit.,* page 129.
[18] *Op. cit.,* page 812.
[19] *Pulpit Commentary on Matthew,* Vol. 2, page 595.

we read thus: "But now is Christ risen from the dead, and become the firstfruits of them that slept.... But every man in his own order: Christ the firstfruits; *afterward they* that are Christ's *at His coming*" (I Cor. 15:20, 23). Note especially, "afterward they that are Christ's at His coming." Christ is the firstfruits. He arose. There is no indication that any others did receive their incorruptible resurrected bodies at that or a later time.

Bishop Nicholson so ably said, "Those Calvary saints went forth from their graves, but only in their natural bodies revived. For the true resurrection body they yet wait till the rising together of all of Christ's from all the ages. No one shall antedate another; no one be perfected before another. God has provided some better thing for us, that those saints out of Calvary graveyard shall not without us be made perfect."[20]

Some may say, "Well, what about Enoch and Elijah? They never saw death. Did they not receive a glorified, incorruptible body such as we shall have?" To this, Bishop Nicholson's answer is appropriate: "If Enoch and Elijah at their translation received the body spiritual, then Christ, Himself, was not the firstfruits."[21] Though Enoch and Elijah were translated, they, in this state, await further experience of a resurrected or incorruptible body like the one all of the Lord's saints shall receive at Christ's coming.

Christ "is the beginning, the firstborn from the dead" (Col. 1:18), or as John wrote, "the first begotten of the dead" (Rev. 1:5). There is none that has preceded Him in resurrection and none have followed Him, and will not until "the trumpet shall sound, and the dead shall be raised incorruptible, and we shall be changed" (I Cor. 15:22). Therefore, I am led to conclude that the saints who came forth from the graves on the first Easter morning came forth, not with incorruptible, eternal bodies, but with bodies that must yet be changed to their glorified state.

---

[20] *Op. cit.*, page 115.
[21] *Ibid.*, page 116.

WHAT HAPPENED TO THEM AFTER THEIR AP-PEARANCE?

When it comes to the consideration as to what happened to the saints who arose after their appearances, we again find that the Scripture is silent. Some feel that they ascended with Christ to heaven when He ascended. Others believe that they died again. The answer to this depends a great deal on the conclusion one derives regarding the nature of the body with which they arose. Those who hold that they came forth from the grave with glorified, incorruptible bodies naturally hold that that they went to heaven with Christ after their mission had been fulfilled. To this writer, this seems to be a straining of the general context and of the over-all teaching of the Bible.

If we can come to an understanding as to the *reason* for their appearance, it may offer a clue as to what happened to them. That they were seen of many is stated by Matthew. It is further stated that it was after the resurrection of Christ that they appeared to the people in the Holy City. It would, therefore, seem evident that these appearances were to sub-stantiate in the hearts of these many witnesses that the resur-rection of Christ was real. "They were permitted," wrote one author, "to show themselves openly in their well known forms to pious relations and friends, as witnesses and proofs of the resurrection."[22]

The "calling back to life" of three different people, as has been recorded for us in the Gospel accounts, was to *prove* that He truly was the Messiah, and, as such, that He had power over death. It is without question that those three whom Christ raised from the dead did not rise with incor-ruptible bodies. Why would it not be the same for the saints who arose when Christ arose as proof that Christ, through His own death, had overcome death and Hades?

Prat contended, "If these privileged ones but had to die again, or if they had recovered their ordinary life at the risk of falling from the beatitude of which they were certain,

[22] *Pulpit Commentary on Matthew*, page 596.

their lot would have in it nothing enviable.[23] To this, I would like to say that if this is so, then Lazarus and the others whom Christ raised from the dead were not blessed either by being brought back to life again. That those whom Christ raised from the dead arose with mortal bodies is certain from the teaching of the Word, for it declares that Christ, Himself, is the "firstfruits of them that slept." So why should not the saints who arose on that Easter day, likewise, return to the grave? To a saint death really holds no terror. They knew the glory of the life beyond the grave. Now that Christ had died and had triumphed over death by His resurrection, to be absent from the body was to be present with the Lord. Therefore, I feel that no injustice could be ascribed to the Lord in raising the saints in mortal bodies.

Many hold that the saints ascended to heaven with Christ instead of returning to the graves. "There can be no doubt, then, that on the day of ascension they formed the escort of the conqueror of death in His triumphal entry into the abode of glory."[24] "This was a resurrection *once for all to life* everlasting; and so there is no room to doubt that they went to glory with the Lord, as bright trophies of His victory over death."[25]

Andrews, though favoring this view, does not state it with any degree of certainty.[26] "Augustine, Theophyluct and others, suppose that these saints died again, while Origen, Jerome, Alford and others, assume that they ascended with Christ to glory.... So much only appears certain to us, that it was a supernatural and symbolic event which proclaimed the truth that the resurrection of Christ was a victory over death and Hades, and opened the door to everlasting life."[27] "Thus, while it was not deemed fitting that He, Himself, should appear again in Jerusalem save to His disciples, pro-

23 *Op. cit.*, page 299.
24 *Ibid.*, page 399.
25 Jamieson, Fausset and Brown, *op. cit.*, page 129.
26 *Op. cit.*, page 547.
27 Schaff, quoted by Lange, *op. cit.*, page 528.

vision was made that the fact of His resurrection should be left in no doubt."[28]

Once the mission of these saints was fulfilled, we know nothing more about them. "When they have demonstrated that the sting was taken from death, that the power of the grave was broken, that men shall rise again with their bodies and be known and recognized, they passed out of sight into the unseen world, and we can follow them no further."[29]

What actually happened to the saints who arose after Christ's resurrection, we are not told. "The whole matter is mysterious and beyond human ken; but we may well believe that this great crisis the Lord, who is the Resurrection and the Life, willed to exemplify His victory over death and to make manifest the resurrection of the body, and this He did by releasing some saintly souls from Hades, and clothed them with the forms in which they had formerly lived, and permitting them to show themselves thus to those who knew and lived then."[30] Bishop Nicholson offered an answer which would seem to be in harmony with the over-all teaching of the Bible. He said, "Possibly the risen saints of our text were afterwards translated, like Enoch and Elijah, in their natural bodies, and did not die again. They may now with Enoch and Elijah, be awaiting the future resurrection. Such a supposition may be true or false. We have no authority for affirming the one or the other; but this we say, that they had not, and have not, the resurrection body of I Corinthians 15."[31] Whatever happened to these saints, whether they were translated like Enoch and Elijah, as Nicholson suggests, or if they again saw death, we know that our Lord is not unjust, and He did that which is in keeping with His holiness and His eternal purpose. The only thing that seems certain is that they had not the resurrected, glorified bodies as they came from the graves.

---

28 Jamieson, Fausset and Brown, *op. cit.*, page 129.
29 *Pulpit Commentary on Matthew*, Vol. 2, page 596.
30 *Ibid.*, page 596.
31 *Op. cit.*, pages 117, 118.

THE TEACHING OF THIS MIRACLE

It happened as "undeniable evidence of ... His resurrection."[32] But, just as there was a spiritual teaching and lesson in each of the preceding miracles, so also in this. Taking the arrangements of the grave clothes as presented in the previous chapter as evidence that He truly arose with a resurrected body, this incident with the saints coming from the graves would seem to teach us that there will be a resurrection of the dead. Jesus, not many days before this, had said, "I am the resurrection and the life: He that believeth in me, though he were dead, yet shall he live" (John 11:25). The saints' resurrection was the immediate proof that He had overcome death, and that the declaration which He had made, "Marvel not at this: for the hour is coming, in the which all that are in the graves shall hear his voice, and shall come forth..." (John 5:28, 29), was true. This miracle, then, would be a sign-proof.

Lange wrote concerning this, "Believers saw persons who had risen from the grave, who had been delivered from Hades. These two facts became one living unity in the Apostle's belief regarding the efficacy of Christ's resurrection. ... The appearances of the bodies may hence be regarded as symbolical; they were the representation of redeemed souls. The death of Christ is accordingly proved at once to be the life of the world; as an atoning death and triumphant entrance into Hades, it acted upon the spirit world, quickening especially Old Testament saints; and these quickened saints reacted by manifold annunciations upon the spiritual conditions of living saints. ... By His death the saints are freed from the bonds of Sheol, by His resurrection, their action on the world is restored."[33]

Lange is trying to indicate that by Christ's death the graves were opened, declaring His victory over Hades, and that by His resurrection we have the assurance that we, too, shall

---

[32] *Critical and Explanatory Commentary,* Vol. 2, page 62.
[33] *Op. cit.,* page 527.

live. This is in agreement with the words of Christ, "Because I live, ye shall live also" (John 14:19) .

Bishop Nicholson said, "Those revived bodies of saints walking the streets of Jerusalem were designed of God as a similitude, a foreshadowing of the life of immortality and eternal glory; but as actual occurrences, they were also a demonstration of the certainty of that of which they were the similitude."[34]

Spurgeon was of the persuasion that the saints who arose at Christ's resurrection "were representative men; they arose as specimens of the way in which all the saints shall in due time arise."[35] This is the position I take as to the real teaching or significance of the resurrection of those saints. They were but a picture or a shadow of the real resurrection that will take place at the time of Christ's second coming. This being the case, it would offer another strong argument against the teaching of some Bible expositors that the saints arose with the incorruptible resurrection bodies. A picture is never the real thing. The Old Testament sacrifices were but a picture or type of the Sacrifice of Christ on the cross. They, however, were not the real sacrifice— they were just a shadow of that which was to come. So also here, the resurrection saints were the *shadow* of the resurrection yet future, which will take place when Christ comes to take the Church, which is His Body, unto Himself.

This great event, recorded only by Matthew, gives us a wonderful hope, which hope "is steadfast and sure." This hope is called the *"blessed hope"* (Titus 2:13) . The glorious appearing of Christ is a blessed hope, because in His coming He will liberate us from the bondage of this flesh and world, and we shall be changed into a body "like unto His glorious body."

Since the teaching of the miracle which we are considering in this chapter teaches us the reality of our resurrection, let us see what the Scriptures have to say about our resurrection. The teaching of this blessed hope is not just confined to the

---

[34] *Op. cit.,* page 121.
[35] Quoted from *Biblical Illustrator on Matthew,* page 662.

New Testament, but is also clearly stated in the inspired pages of the Old Testament. We have the familiar testimony and witness of Job, who said, "For I know that my Redeemer liveth, and that he shall stand at the latter day upon the earth: and though after my skin, worms destroy this body, yet in my flesh shall I see God: Whom I shall see for myself, and mine eyes shall behold, and not another; though my reins be consumed within me" (Job 19:25-27). The Prophet Isaiah declared, "Thy dead men shall live, together with my dead body shall they arise. Awake and sing, ye that dwell in the dust" (Isa. 26:19).

Jesus very emphatically declared the truth of a physical resurrection from the grave. He said, "Marvel not at this: for the hour is coming, in the which all that are in the graves shall hear his voice, and shall come forth: they that have done good, unto the resurrection of life; and they that have done evil, unto the resurrection of damnation" (John 5:28, 29).

The Sadducees in the days of Christ contested the doctrine of the resurrection, but when Christ came forth from the grave, He brought proof with Him that resurrection not only was possible, but that it was real. It was a picture of what Paul records for us in the great resurrection chapter of the Bible, "Behold, I show you a mystery; we shall not all sleep, but we shall all be changed, in a moment, in the twinkling of an eye, at the last trump: for the trumpet shall sound, and the dead shall be raised incorruptible, and we shall be changed. For this corruptible must put on incorruption, and this mortal must put on immortality" (I Cor. 15:51-53). "For the Lord himself shall descend from heaven with a shout, with the voice of the archangel, and with the trump of God: and the dead in Christ shall rise first. Then we which are alive and remain shall be caught up together with them in the clouds, to meet the Lord in the air: and so shall we ever be with the Lord" (I Thess. 4:16, 17).

The future resurrection will be as real as the resurrection of Christ, Himself. At that resurrection He "shall change our vile body, that it may be fashioned like unto his glorious body, according to the working whereby he is able even to subdue all things unto himself" (Phil. 3:21). Another statement that teaches us that our body will be fashioned like unto His body is given to us by John. "Beloved, now are we the sons of God, and it doth not yet appear what we shall be: but we know that, when he shall appear, *we shall be like him; for we shall see him as he is*" (I John 3:2).

However, not all that are brought forth from the graves will come forth with glorified bodies. Jesus said, "they that have done good to the resurrection of life." This is the resurrection of glory, but He continued, "but they that have done evil unto the resurrection of damnation" (John 5:29). These are the ones who have counted the Blood of Christ as an unholy thing, and have done despite to the Spirit of Grace. What greater evil could one do than to ignore or reject the love and grace of our Lord! The above statement of Christ is in agreement with the words of Paul who said, "For as in Adam all die, even so in Christ shall *all* be made alive" (I Cor. 15:22). But Revelation 20:4-6 reveals that there is a period of a thousand years which will elapse between the first resurrection, which is the resurrection of the just, and the resurrection of the damned. The damned are those whose names have never been recorded in the Lamb's Book of Life through faith in the sacrificial death of Christ on the cross and His triumphant resurrection. Their resurrection will be one in which they will hear the words of our Lord as He sits on the great white throne, "Depart from me ye workers of iniquity," to be cast into the lake of fire.

In the light of this, is it any wonder that "we look for the *Saviour, the Lord Jesus Christ*"? This is our hope, and was assured to us in that many saints were raised from the dead on the day Christ arose from the grave.

> "We shall sleep, but not forever,
>   There will be a glorious dawn!
> We shall meet, to part — no, never,
>   On the resurrection morn!
> From the deepest caves of ocean,
>   From the desert and the plain,
> From the valley and the mountain,
>   Countless throngs shall rise again.

"We shall sleep, but not forever,
    In the lone and silent grave;
Blessed be the Lord that taketh,
    Blessed be the Lord that gave.
In the bright Eternal City
    Death can never, never come!
In His own good time He'll call us
    From our rest to Home, sweet Home!"
                    — Mary Ann Kidder

Summary

It is difficult to summarize, in a few pages, the over-all teaching of these seven great miracles of Golgotha. Basically, I believe that we see in it the declaration of the wonderful and supernatural character of the One who had been crucified.

1. The darkness, which preceded His death, was not caused by a natural eclipse because it is impossible to have an eclipse of the sun when the moon is full. This was the case on the Passover day when Christ was crucified. This darkness, which possibly covered the entire earth, was symbolical of the darkness through which Christ was going for the whole world of mankind. We see in it an expression of God's extreme displeasure against sin. Jesus was, here, taking the judgment (of which darkness is a Biblical symbol) for sin upon Himself. It illustrated the suffering He endured, the darkness of being forsaken by the Father, and becoming the very curse itself. Here, He tasted for all men the awfulness of being lost — forsaken by God. What could better portray this than darkness?

We, as redeemed mankind, will never know by experience the real meaning of the darkness on Golgotha. For us the darkness is past — it was placed on the sinless Son of God — we have only glory awaiting us.

2. The rest of the miracles that followed happened after the awful, agonizing death. The moment His life expired, or He dismissed His spirit, the veil in the temple was rent in two from the top to the bottom. So momentous and significant an occurrence as the rending of the veil made a tremendous impact upon the people of that day. The rending of the veil was an act of God, whereby He declared that all

that the veil had signified had been fulfilled by the One who had just died on Golgotha's Hill. The veil had shut man out from the presence of God. Now, in the name of this Sufferer, whose death caused the rent, access to God is possible for all who come to Him in faith. At one time it was death to go into the presence of God. Now it is death to stay out.

The rent veil declared the end of symbolic worship and from that time on worship was to be in spirit and in truth. The Law (of which the veil spoke) had been fulfilled, thus a new era or dispensation was begun. Man now had free access to God without any other human priest to represent him before the one and only Holy God.

3. The earthquake was another miracle to show that Jesus was truly the promised Messiah. Evidences of such an earthquake are supposed to be visable today in the surrounding area of Jerusalem.

This earthquake was a symbol of triumph and victory. The Law, which had been introduced by an earthquake, was declared to have been fulfilled by the same token. This earthquake, which rent the rocks, was earth's response to the triumphant shout of Jesus. Just as the earth had shared in the curse of sin, so the earth is to share in the victories of the Crucified.

The graves were opened to show that through death, Christ had overcome him that had the power of death. This declared that a resurrection was to follow.

4. When the side of Jesus Christ was pierced with the sword by a Roman soldier, blood and water came forth from the gash. I believe that it was literally *blood* and *water*. There is no natural explanation for it. It was simply another miracle to show forth by symbol the mission for which He had come.

Simply stated, this miracle teaches us that Christ came, not only to redeem man from the curse or consequences of sin, but also to make it possible for man to walk in the newness of life, cleansed daily by the washing of the water. How thankful we should be for the fountain filled with blood, which washes and cleanses from every sin and stain!

5. Since Jesus is truly the Son of God, it was impossible that He should be holden of death. It had been promised by the prophets that His body should not see corruption, and thus He came forth from the grave, the victor.

Those who deny the bodily resurrection of Jesus Christ must account for the missing body and the boldness of the witnesses of that day who bravely bore the testimony of this truth, — even at the cost of their own lives.

If Christ is not risen, then all our hope is useless, and we are yet in our sins. We, however, have the sure promises of the Word of God and the witness of the Holy Spirit within that Jesus Christ is alive today. He is even at the right hand of God, there serving as our Advocate.

6. One of the greatest outward evidences offered to us for the resurrection of Christ is given to us by John in his Gospel account. He said that, when he saw the grave clothes, he believed in the physical resurrection of Jesus. It was the fact that the body of Jesus Christ had come forth from the grave clothes without disturbing them in their original convolutions that made John come to the conclusion that the miracle of the resurrection had taken place.

7. The revival to life of many saints after Christ's resurrection has in it an element of mystery. Though the account is only a brief statement, it is nevertheless true — as is all of Scripture.

We have here the symbolic declaration that the risen Christ is truly the Lord of life, and that He will, as He has promised, some day call forth from the graves *all* who throughout the ages have been buried, whether in the earth or in the sea.

The controversy over who these saints were does not do away with the fact as stated. It seems evident that these saints came forth with revived bodies and must have returned to the graves after their mission was completed.

CONCLUSION: In these miracles we see that all the needs of lost mankind have been met, beginning with the substitutionary death for our sins, on through this life to the day when we shall be raised from the dead to be made like unto the resurrected Son of God.

> " 'Man of sorrow,' what a name
> For the Son of God who came
> Ruined sinners to reclaim!
> Hallelujah! what a Saviour!"
> — P. P. Bliss

Bibliography

Andrews, Samuel J., *The Life of Our Lord upon the Earth,* Charles Scribner's Sons, New York, 1867

Appleton, George, *John's Witness to Jesus,* Association Press, New York, 1955

Barnes, Albert, *Barnes' Notes on the New Testament* on Matthew and Mark, Baker Book House, Grand Rapids, Michigan, 1949

Besser, Wilhelm Friedrich, *The Passion Story (Die Leidensgeshichte),* Augsburg Publishing House, Minneapolis, 1847 (English Translation, 1953)

Clarke, Adam, *Clarke's Commentary,* Vol V, Abingdon Press, Nashville

Edersheim, Alfred, *The Life and Times of Jesus the Messiah,* Vol. II, William B. Eerdmans Publishing Co., Grand Rapids, Michigan, 1947

Evans, William, *The Great Doctrines of the Bible,* The Bible Institute Association, Chicago, 1912

Exell, Joseph S., *The Biblical Illustrator* on Matthew, Baker Book House, Grand Rapids, Michigan, 1951

Farrar, Frederic W., *The Life of Christ,* George H. Doran Co., New York, 1876

Gould, Ezra P., *The International Critical Commentary* on Mark, T. & T. Clark, Edinburgh, 1896

Gray, James C., and Adams, George M., *Bible Commentary,* Vol. IV, Zondervan Publishing House, Grand Rapids, Michigan

Haines, Perry F., *The Jesus Paul Preached,* W. A. Wilde Company, Boston, 1949

Hastings, James, *A Dictionary of the Bible,* Vol. I, Charles Scribner's Sons, New York, 1900

Hendriksen, William, *New Testament Commentary* on the Gospel of John, Vol. II, Baker Book House, Grand Rapids, Michigan, 1954

Henry, Matthew, *Commentary on the Whole Bible,* Vol. V, Fleming H. Revell Co., Westwood, New Jersey, 1925

Hill William Bancroft, *The Resurrection of Jesus Christ,* Fleming H. Revell Co., Westwood, New Jersey, 1930

Humberd, R. I., *Many Infallible Proofs,* Christian Book Depot, Flora, Indiana

Jamieson, Fausset and Brown, *A Commentary, Critical, Experimental and Practical,* Vols. V and VII, William B. Eerdmans Publishing Co., Grand Rapids, Mich., 1945

Krummacher, F. W., *The Suffering Saviour,* Moody Press, Chicago, 1948

Lange, J. P., *The Life of the Lord Jesus Christ,* Vol. III (Gospels) , T. & T. Clark, Edinburgh, 1872

Lange, J. P., *Lange's Commentary, Critical, Doctrinal and Homiletical,* on Matthew and John (Trans. by Philip Schaff) , Charles Scribner's Sons, New York, 1905

Lenski R. C. H., *The Interpretation of Saint John's Gospel,* The Lutheran Book Concern, Columbus, Ohio, 1942

Lenski, R. C. H., *The Interpretation of Saint Mark's Gospel,* The Wartburg Press, Columbus, Ohio, 1943

MacGregor, G. H. C., *The Gospel of John,* Harper and Bros., New York, n.d.

Maclaren, Alexander, *Exposition of Holy Scriptures,* Vol. VII, William B. Eerdmans Publishing Co., Grand Rapids, Michigan, 1952

McCaulay, J. C., *Devotional Studies in St. John's Gospel,* William B. Eerdmans Publishing Co., Grand Rapids, Michigan, 1949

Meyer, A. W., *Critical and Exegetical Commentary on the New Testament,* The Gospel of John, Vol. II, Funk and Wagnalls, New York, 1891

Morgan, G. Campbell, *The Gospel According to Matthew, The Gospel According to John,* Fleming H. Revell Company, Westwood, New Jersey, 1929

Nicholson, William R., *The Six Miracles of Calvary*, Moody
    Press, Chicago, 1927

Orr, James, *The Resurrection of Jesus*, George H. Doran Co.,
    New York

Plummer, Alfred, *The International Critical Commentary* on
    Luke, T. & T. Clark, Edinburgh, 1896

Prat, Ferdinand, *Jesus and His Life, His Teaching and His
    His Work*, Vol. II., Bruce Publishing Co., Milwaukee, 1950

Strong, James, *A Concise Dictionary of the Words in the
    Hebrew Bible*, Abingdon Press, Nashville, 1890

Thayer, Joseph H., *Greek-English Lexicon of the New Testa-
    ment*, American Book Co., New York, 1956

*A Preacher's Homiletical Commentary on the Gospel of
    Matthew*, Funk and Wagnalls Co., New York, 1892

*An Exegetical Commentary on the Gospel According to Mat-
    thew*, William B. Eerdman's Publishing Co., Grand Rapids,
    Michigan, 1953

An Exposition of the Bible, Vol. IV and V., The S. S. Scran-
    ton Co., Hartford, Connecticut, 1911.

International Standard Bible Encyclopedia, Vols. I, II, and
    V, William B. Eerdmans Publishing Co., Grand Rapids,
    Michigan, 1947

Life and Work of Flavius Josephus, The John C. Winston
    Co., Philadelphia, n.d.

Pulpit Commentary, on Matthew, Vol. II, and Mark, Vol. II.
    Funk and Wagnalls Co., New York

The Interpreter's Bible, Vol. VII and VIII, Abingdon Press,
    Nashville

The Moffatt New Testament Commentary, Harper and
    Brothers, New York

Westcott, B. F., *The Gospel According to St. John*, William
    B. Eerdmans Publishing Co., Grand Rapids, Michigan,
    1950

Index of Scripture Texts